Implementing

the code of practice

for children with

special educational needs

A practical guide

Second Edition

AHMAD F. RAMJHUN

David Fulton Publishers
London

David Fulton Publishers Ltd
The Chiswick Centre, 414 Chiswick High Road, London W4 5TF

First edition published in Great Britain by David Fulton Publishers Ltd 1995
Second edition 2002

British Library Cataloguing in Publication Data
A catalogue record for this book is available from the British Library.

ISBN 1-85346-663-8

Typeset by Servis Filmsetting Ltd, Manchester
Printed in Great Britain by Bell & Bain Ltd, Glasgow

Contents

Foreword

We have come a long way from the days when many children with special educational needs were left to sink or swim (too often to sink) or were consigned to segregated places in remote – and too often unpleasant – parts of the school. Now, most children and young people with special educational needs are assessed carefully and there are well-focused plans which support their learning; generating progress which secures their place among their peers and, ultimately, as fully functioning adults in society. However, we still need to be vigilant. There are still young people whose needs are not properly recognised, let alone assessed and provided for. There are others who are given special treatment but who make much less progress than they might because a ceiling is placed on expectations. The key to getting it right lies in the Code of Practice, a ground-breaking protocol which defines what is needed to support all young people with special educational needs.

The first edition of Ahmad's book has supported hundreds of teachers and parents in meeting young people's special educational needs. Now he has brought his rich experience as a local education authority officer to bear on the new Code of Practice to revise his practical guide. It gives invaluable support to those who have to implement the Code, both as a reminder to those who have been working with special educational needs for a long time, and as an introduction to those who are starting out on doing so for the first time.

Ian Sandbrook
Executive Director
Lifelong Learning and Leisure
Southampton City Council
May 2002

Acknowledgements

Since the first publication of my work on the Code of Practice for Children with Special Educational Needs, I have continued to be actively involved in researching how children's needs can best be met in the context of schools and other settings. I have been impressed with the enormous skills and expertise which exist, particularly with the commitment to promoting children's best interests. I hope that all these colleagues who work so hard on children's behalf will have their contributions recognised and celebrated.

Nearer home, I would like to thank my own colleagues within Southampton LEA who are, without doubt, children's champions. I would like to mention Peter Lewis, Assistant Director of Education, and Peter Sharp, until recently, Principal Educational Psychologist. They have been hugely influential in my learning and practice. So too have colleagues within my own team and I would like to thank them; they have worked tirelessly in helping me promote and secure best practice.

Finally, I would like to record my warmest appreciation and gratitude to my family and friends. My two children have been solid in their support of me in my efforts to combine my responsibilties of being a parent with those of a professional practitioner who never seems to stop working. This book is dedicated to them with love.

Ahmad F. Ramjhun
Southampton
March 2002

Preface

Education in this country has been subject to fierce and rapid changes over the past two decades. The pace has been relentless. Claims have been made about 'falling standards' in spite of the lack of evidence and political attempts made to put right the perceived inadequacies in the system. This started with the now famous 'Ruskin' speech made by James Callaghan in 1986, followed by various legislation to centralise control (see Evans and Tomlinson 1989). Teachers have borne the brunt of the criticisms, not all justified or warranted, being seen to have failed to raise standards and to prepare children for their future role as citizens and providers for the nation. There followed attempts, some well intentioned and others misguided, to grasp control over schools and to determine the education provided to children (Booth 1994, Galloway *et al.* 1994). The autonomy of the teaching profession has been progressively dismantled with a series of central education initiatives to implement the requirements of the Education Reform Act 1988; for example, the introduction of the National Curriculum and key stage tests.

Of particular significance was the setting up of the Office for Standards in Education (Ofsted) whose primary role was to inspect schools to ensure that standards were being met. This had direct impact on raising teacher accountability; schools performing badly were found either to have serious weaknesses or to require 'special measures', the latter being the weaker category where intensive support was deemed to be needed. Those which failed to respond to such support were closed. By 2002, all schools had been inspected and league tables published based on their pupil performance at each key stage and particularly at GCSE. Her Majesty's Chief Inspector, in his 2002 annual report (Ofsted 2002), claimed that standards had risen significantly in all schools; of lessons observed, very few were unsatisfactory. However, he also recognised severe teacher shortages and the impact these were likely to have in the classroom. The government's agenda to promote the inclusion of children experiencing learning difficulties in mainstream settings (DfEE 1997, DfES 2001a, 2001b) is bearing a great deal of the blame. Disruptive behaviour, in particular, is claimed to be driving teachers out of classrooms (Parsons 2000) though it is more likely that decades of unrelenting political onslaught have made this profession less attractive, having removed its autonomy and control in the classroom.

Central government had assumed control of the curriculum in the late 1980s, resulting in the imposition of a National Curriculum to be followed by all state schools and prescribed in great detail, initially with little room for teachers and others responsible for its implementation to manoeuvre. Legislation in the form of the 1988 Education Act was passed by the Conservative Government, requiring the study of core subjects by all children and prescribing standard assessments at key stages of children's schooling, i.e. at 7, 11, 14, and 16. Considerable controversy ensued, amid resistance from the teacher unions, forcing a reconsideration of the issues and the tasks expected of teachers. The end result has been a slimmed down version of the National Curriculum and increased teacher flexibility in recognition of their responsibilities and superior knowledge of the child in their class (see the Dearing Report (DfEE 1994)). Key Stage 4 flexibility has been welcomed, particularly as other challenges have increased; for example, increased competition in the education market-place, the publication of league tables and the introduction of the literacy hour and numeracy hour.

Children with special educational needs had also been the subject of detailed attention, resulting in far-reaching changes in the way they are viewed and educated. The Warnock Report on the Education of Children with Special Educational Needs (1978) inspired new thinking and a radically different approach to the concept of special need. Children were no longer to be categorised into groups for learning difficulties and the focus was no longer on their disability. Rather, the emphasis was on children's needs and the help they require to make progress in learning.

The 1981 Education Act incorporated the recommendations of the Warnock Committee. The Act was not implemented in local education authorities (LEAs) until April 1983 and had a mixed reception among schools, LEAs, parents and central government. Its Achilles' heel was the cost to education providers and the number of appeals that arose through conflict from perceived inadequacies to provide for children in need. It was therefore inevitable that it would be revised and repealed by new legislation. This came about in the form of the 1993 Education Act, much of which concentrates on Grant Maintained Status for schools. Part 3, however, is specifically concerned with the education of children with special educational needs. This details the requirements of the assessment and review procedures and requires the provision of a Code of Practice to provide guidance to LEAs, Health Trusts, Social Services Departments and schools on how to discharge their responsibilities with regard to children experiencing special educational needs.

The original Code of Practice was a comprehensive document, approved by Parliament in 1994. It came into effect in September 1994 and all parties in education were required to have regard to its guidance. That Code and its successor are the result of legislation and are pursuant to the 1993, 1996 and 2001 Education Acts respectively. The revised Code, which came into force in January 2002, continues to provide a useful source of reference though it is constrained by a statutory framework that could be argued to be dating (see Chapter 1).

This book on the implementation of the revised Code of Practice arises from a perceived need for teachers, LEA officers, governors and parents and the voluntary agencies to have a practical and accessible guide to help them discharge their key duties and responsibilities. It details the key changes that have been made to the original code and their implications for practice. The core of the text is written primarily with teachers and education support staff in mind, though parents, governors and staff from both statutory and voluntary agencies will find the content equally useful.

Chapter 1 presents an overview of the Code. Chapter 2 summarises the key revisions, and Chapter 3 details its implications for the class teacher in primary and secondary schools. Chapter 4 focuses on the roles of governing bodies and includes guidance on the preparation of schools' Special Educational Needs Policies. Chapter 5 deals with the preparation of Individual Education Plans (IEPs) and provides guidance on their preparation and completion, including a section on a selection of problem-solving strategies which teachers will find useful. Chapter 6 deals with the new emphasis on School Action and School Action Plus. These replace the 'stages' of identification and intervention in the original Code (see DfE 1994, Ramjhun 1995). Chapter 6 details the process, requirements and responsibilities during School Action and School Action Plus. Chapter 7 describes the statutory process and discusses criteria for statutory assessment, including guidance on how to prepare the Educational Advice (now renamed as Appendix B). Chapters 8 and 9 concentrate on the Annual Review procedures and the Transition Plan which is produced for a student at 14+ years of age. Chapter 10 deals with parents' rights, roles and responsibilities, the principles of partnership, and the requirement to ensure that children's voices are heard. Chapter 10 provides some views and reflections on the workings of the Special Educational Needs Tribunal. These are views aimed at the educational practioner who might be faced with the need to appear at a Tribunal as a key witness for either the LEA or parents. The emphasis is on offering advice and guidance on its proceedings and procedures; legal issues are not covered as these are outside the scope of this work.

A recurring theme throughout the book is the need to ascertain and include the child's perspective, in addition to the views of the parents. Parents are also encouraged to include the views of the family where this is relevant. It is firmly held that the starting point with any teaching activity should be the child, whether or not the child has special needs. Every child is different, so there is no panacea or cure-all; the advice is know your child and do not assume that problems that appear similar are the same. Much will depend on the creativity and insight of the teacher but no progress will be made until and unless the child is actively engaged. This implies a number of requirements, among which the most important are to gain the child's trust and confidence, to build and develop a mutually satisfying relationship and to enable cooperation. If parents are also brought in as active partners, this makes for a more effective and planned approach, ensuring consistency and coherence which can only be to the good.

The convention adopted in this book is to use the masculine 'he' when referring to a child. This is in order to avoid the cumbersome usage of he/she to refer to children and no discrimination is intended in any way. This book is not intended to be other than a practical guide to the Code of Practice. The only authoritative version is the Code itself which has Parliamentary approval. Therefore, reference should be made to the Code for specific guidance where doubts exist or to the 2001 Education Act and the associated regulations for points of law. The views expressed in this work are the author's and do not necessarily represent those of Southampton City Council.

I hope this book guides you through the effective implementation of the SEN Code of Practice.

Purpose

The purpose of this handbook is to enable the reader to:

- understand and implement the requirements of the Code of Practice with regard to children experiencing special educational needs
- discharge their duties and responsibilities at each stage of their work and with specific reference to the Code
- follow best practice in working with and supporting children experiencing difficulties in learning

Audience

This handbook is intended as a resource for:

- teachers and special needs assistants in schools, whether or not they work directly with a child experiencing special educational needs
- headteachers and special needs coordinators whose task is to ensure implementation and facilitation of the Code in their schools
- governing bodies whose responsibilities are to ensure that their schools are having regard to the Code
- LEA officers, psychologists, health and social services staff who have a part to play in the implementation of the Code
- parents who will also find this handbook useful in identifying the duties placed on schools and others when providing for their child's special educational needs. It will help clarify the roles and responsibilities of the various staff who work with their children, the procedures to be followed and the documentation to be kept; it will also help them to understand their role when working in partnership with the various agencies

Overview

This handbook sets out to answer the following questions:

What is the Code of Practice about? (*Chapter 1*)
What are the key changes that have been made? (*Chapter 2*)
As a member of staff in a school, what do I need to know and do? (*Chapter 3*)
As a governor, what do I need to know and do? (*Chapter 4*)
How are good IEPs produced? (*Chapter 5*)
What do I need to know about School Action and School Action Plus? (*Chapter 6*)
How do I get through the maze called 'statutory assessment'? (*Chapter 7*)
How do I make the best of the Annual Review? (*Chapter 8*)
How do I write a good Transition Plan? (*Chapter 9*)
What do I as a parent need to know about the Code? (*Chapter 10*)

List of abbreviations

ACE	Advisory Centre for Education
AT	Attainment Target
CMO	Clinical Medical Officer or School Doctor
DES	Department of Education and Science
DFE	Department for Education
DfEE	Department for Education and Employment
DfES	Department for Education and Skills
EP	Educational Psychologist
FEFC	Further Education Funding Council
IEP	Individual Education Plan
LEA	Local Education Authority
LSA	Learning Support Assistant
LSC	Learning Skills Council
NC	National Curriculum
NVQ	National Vocational Qualification
Ofsted	Office for Standards in Education
PEST	A problem-solving technique which examines the political, economic, social and technological aspects of problems/issues
QTA	Qualified Teacher Assistant
SEN	Special Educational Needs
SENCO	SEN Co-ordinator
SENDIST	Special Educational Needs and Disability Tribunal
SNA	Special Needs Assistant
STA	Specialist Teacher Adviser (for a type of learning difficulty)
SWOT	Strengths, Weaknesses, Opportunities and Threats analysis
TA	Teaching Assistant

1 An introduction to the Code of Practice

Introduction to handbook

This handbook is a revision of the guidance produced in 1995 when the original 1994 Code of Practice came into force (Ramjhun 1995). It summarises the key changes that have been made to this Code, including my interpretations and reflections where appropriate. I was a member of the group convened under the auspices of NAGSEN, the National Advisory Group on Special Educational Needs, to assist in this revision. This sub-group represented a wide range of interests, from parents to specialist interest groups and LEA officer representatives. This enabled wide-ranging discussion of issues with a common and shared objective of furthering the interests of children experiencing difficulties in learning.

The main constraint facing the sub-group derived from the statutory framework, the risk being that only minor changes would be acceptable. However, there appeared to be a commitment to addressing some of the issues raised from the implementation of the 1994 Code, particularly the need to reduce bureaucracy and to review the role and function of the SEN tribunal. Some of these required new regulations, e.g. extending parental rights of appeal in respect of school requests for statutory assessment and placing time limits on LEAs to implement tribunal orders. Others required amendments to the 1996 Education Act, e.g. Section 316 was revised to strengthen children's rights to mainstream education. However, there were also many opportunities missed to bring the Code up to date with other education developments, particularly those linked with inclusive thinking. Although inclusion features in the new Code, it sits uncomfortably in it. This is because the Code still emphasises the 'special needs pupil' discourse; there is very little said about teacher or school effectiveness, or indeed 'disability rights' matters which are more directly and fundamentally linked to inclusion. It is as if the Code ignores decades of research showing the links between schools and the barriers that they can present to pupil participation (see Galloway *et al.* 1994, Reynolds 1995). Warnings about the outdated nature of the concept of special needs also appear to have gone largely unheeded. Only recently, Mittler (2000) was arguing for the abandonment of the language of special needs that 'create or maintain mindsets that perpetuate segregation at the very time when we are talking about moving towards a more inclusive education system and a more inclusive society. In this context, the continued use of special is not only anachronistic but discriminatory' (p. 8). Corbett (1996) had also referred to 'bad mouthing' in the language of special education, arguing that reference to needs signals dependency, inadequacy and lack of worth.

An equally serious shortcoming is the new Code's failure to deal with the issue of assessment. Although it provides extensive details of the processes and procedures of assessment, it fails to address the tensions that research has consistently shown to arise from the process. Galloway *et al.* (1994) had already shown how statutory assessment directly affects the hopes and expectations of its participants and how these are further compounded by policy constraints at school, LEA or government levels. Perhaps the revised Code should have clarified the roles and responsibilities of each participant, especially those with a duty to make the special educational provision or to facilitate other outcomes of the assessment. There is still too much confusion over who provides for the majority of children experiencing difficulties in learning; do schools provide for Warnock's 18 per cent and LEAs for the remaining 2 per cent with Statements of SEN? Since local management of schools (LMS), teachers have become increasingly used to LEAs taking responsibility for the funding of SEN (Bowers *et al.* 1988); however, as more SEN resources are being delegated, greater clarity is now required with regard to school functions in this area. Although 'School Action' and 'School Action Plus' are introduced, the new Code does not make sufficient use of the opportunity presented to deal with this issue.

It took nearly two years to revise the 1994 Code of Practice for Children with SEN. The end result was little more than a revision; much of the original thinking and creativity that could have added to this was incorporated in an SEN Toolkit (DfES 2001b) which was published at the same time. The latter is likely to stimulate innovations and change in schools; it was able to be more comprehensive and, more importantly, did not have to stick too rigidly to the existing statutory framework. On reflection, it seems to me that it is probably the statutory framework that needed revising and not the Code of Practice. Basing a revised code on old legislation was probably a mistake; there have been so many changes in education and at such a fast pace that, other than a complete rewrite, a revised code would be an anachronism on the day it came into force. Yet it will continue to be a key and essential reference in any SEN tribunal or court of law. Let us hope that the focus will be on its accomplishments and improvements, not its limitations. Like many colleagues who helped with its revision, my aspirations are that the revised Code will continue to serve the interests of children experiencing difficulties in learning for the next decade or at least until such time as it is rewritten to retain its strengths and reframe its focus away from its individualised to a more inclusive approach.

Background to the 1994 Code of Practice

It can be said that the 1994 Code of Practice was introduced in order to put right some of the deficiencies perceived to have arisen since the implementation of the 1981 Education Act. Most notable of these were the criticisms which had been made by the Audit Commission in their reports *Getting in on the Act* and *Getting the Act Together* (Audit Commission/HMI 1992a and 1992b).

These were linked to the lack of accountability by some schools in their use of resources allocated for children experiencing special educational needs. The main problem here was that some schools failed to specify exactly how resources had been targeted to support children experiencing difficulties in learning. Conspicuous amongst this was an absence of details relating to teaching programmes and their organisation and implementation, including the staff allocation needed. There had been unacceptably long delays by LEAs to process the statutory assessment of children experiencing special educational needs.

The Audit Commission found that the majority of LEAs were taking far too long to complete the statutory assessment procedures, under the terms of the 1981 Education Act. This ranged from a few months to a few years, revealing inconsistencies between LEAs and raising suspicion among parents and pressure groups that the procedures were being used as delaying tactics.

The making of Statements of special educational needs was considered too vague, lacking in specificity and clarity relating to objectives and provision, making these weak and potentially liable to abuse. This was a common observation, particularly from the recipients of Statements, and also reinforced by the Audit Commission. The main criticisms have been that the child's special educational needs have tended, on the whole, not to be clearly specified. There were occasionally failures to specify each and every need (i.e. the 'Dorset judgment' 1991) and a lack of specificity relating to the provision needed, including some confusion as to exactly *who* should be funding specialist resources, such as speech therapy (i.e. the 'Oxford judgment'). (See Denman and Lunt (1993) for a review of cases which have gone to judicial review.)

The number of appeals reaching the Secretary of State had increased and there was a perceived need to bring consistency and fairness in regard to Appeal Committees' recommendations, leading to their replacement with the new Special Educational Needs Tribunals. The main concern was the inability of the Appeals Committees to enforce their recommendations on LEAs, as the latter could choose to ignore them – leaving the only recourse for parents being to appeal to the Secretary of State. This was compounded no doubt by the lack of consistency of Appeal Committees and the possible role conflict of local councillors sitting on them, the conflicting roles being loyalty to their LEAs as elected representatives and their obligation to safeguard children's best interests. This raised doubts about objectivity and impartiality (Chasty and Friel 1991, Robinson 1994, DFE 1994).

It was therefore inevitable that legislation would be undertaken in an attempt to resolve these issues. Part III of the 1993 Education Act tried to address these concerns. This it did by repealing most of the 1981 Education Act and by making specific provisions for each of the above, including the requirement for a Code of Practice to be produced to secure practical guidance to LEAs and others with responsibility for children experiencing special educational needs (see Robinson 1994).

Issues since 1994

Since 1994, some of the above issues have continued to cause concern. The revised Code was delayed because it had sought to remove the requirement for SEN provision to be specified and quantified. It had become apparent that there was no requirement in previous law for this degree of specification and quantification although it had been raised in the 1994 Code of Practice. A high court judgment had, however, found in favour of parents who had sought such specificity against an SEN tribunal which had considered that some flexibility was required where appropriate (Somerset judgment 2000). The proposed revised Code that was eventually passed in Parliament re-included this requirement for specificity while still managing to retain the principle that flexibility will be desirable at times.

Similarly, the issue of speech and language therapy has continued to be unresolved. This is in spite of the setting up of a working party to address the way forward (see DfEE 2000a). Although since previous court rulings, e.g. the Lancashire and Harrow judgments, speech and language therapy has been regarded as largely educational provision, there has been little progress on who should fund this, though the duty remains with LEAs. Government's expectation was that the flexibilities of the Health Act 1990 would allow closer partnerships between LEAs and health agencies for this purpose but local variations in practice have meant that some health authorities have not deemed speech and language therapy as a health priority so that the funding has not been forthcoming. The point being missed is that children do not need speech and language therapy; they need a combination of education and language intervention programmes to develop their communication skills. These are not within the skills and expertise of speech and language therapists alone; they require a multidisciplinary approach within which the speech and language therapist plays only a small part. Integral within such teams are teachers, LSAs, children's parents and their peers who have a crucial and enriching role. Yet many tribunal and court appeals have focused exclusively on speech and language therapy as if that was the only requirement.

Other issues have tended to be around teacher workloads and a tendency for the Individual Education Plan (IEP) and Annual Review processes to be unnecessarily bureaucratic and unwieldy (see Ofsted 1996, Bowers *et al.* 1998). However, the most troubling to parents and LEAs has been the dramatic rise in tribunal appeals. Far from reducing the need for conflict and appeals, the 1994 Code led to many appeals, confirming the need for mediation and conciliation. Such need was not recognised in 1994 but is becoming alarmingly evident.

It is interesting that the Department for Education and Skills (DfES) and the revised Code seeks conciliation services independent of the LEA. Lord Woolf defines mediation as involving a neutral intermediary who encourages the parties to reach an agreed settlement using 'shuttle diplomacy' to bring the two sides to an agreement. Conciliation uses a similar process to mediation, but the conciliator plays a more proactive role, and may suggest settlement terms (see Freshfields Litigation Team 1998: 15). Conciliation lies as an extension of parent partnership services outside of LEAs and is a recognition that current levels of services are not working as tribunal appeals continue to rise. Whether they will make any difference is debatable; the road to tribunal may still remain the most promising to many parents. The cure for dealing with conflicts is not to introduce a legal requirement for conciliation; this is not without further costs, resources which should have been more appropriately directed to schools. Tribunals, parent partnership and conciliation services are costly and will involve millions of pounds of expenditure. Do these, however, reflect the truer focus, that these services are politically attractive and meet the needs of parents and not necessarily those of children? Central government's strategy seems to be to pass legislation and to make further expectations of LEAs which it has striven to weaken over the years and for which it seems to be reserving the role of dealing with conflicts arising out of SEN casework. Perhaps, the focus should have been about managing the problem of assessment and the demand and expectations that this creates more forcefully and honestly. Exactly what are the criteria for statutory assessment? Whose needs do they serve? How should these be funded? What changes are expected: in children; in adult providers; in schools? What are success criteria and how will these represent best value? I am not sure that the Code answers any of these in any depth.

The original 1994 Code of Practice: an overview

The original Code of Practice came into effect in September 1994. It was a requirement of the 1993 Education Act, calling on the Secretary of State to provide practical guidance to Local Education Authorities (LEAs), schools and other agencies, namely Social Services Departments and Health Trusts, on how to discharge their responsibilities with regard to children who experience special educational needs.

The 1994 Code represented a significant milestone in special needs thinking at the time and provided detailed and comprehensive guidance on the procedures to be followed on the identification and assessment of children who experience special educational needs and the planning, teaching and provision to meet those needs. It detailed the responsibilities of LEAs, schools, Health Services and Social Services Departments to work in partnership with each other and with parents, in their responses to children experiencing special educational needs.

The Code provided a framework to inform and support practices to help children experiencing special educational needs and built on the principles first set out in the 1981 Education Act. In common with other legislation, e.g. the National Curriculum, it included a certain amount of prescription, particularly with regard to procedures, but left some flexibility with the processes – for example, in relation to formal criteria for statutory assessment, and schools' decisions on their special educational needs policies, allocation of special educational needs resources and organisational arrangements.

There were clear and specific expectations, some setting out precisely the stages to be followed in assessment and minimum requirements relating to matters such as consultation with parents and involvement of outside agencies.

Other requirements were more focused on the need for prompt and effective response within statutory time limits, especially on the statutory assessment of children, LEAs being required to complete the process within 26 weeks. The procedures relating to Annual Reviews were detailed, as were parental rights and expectations, particularly the time to be allowed for parents to study reports, professional advice and/or evidence prior to Annual Reviews. The time limits between 14+ reviews and the receipt of Transition Plans were also specified.

The 1994 Code, however, was not explicit on criteria for statutory assessment and asserts that indeed it could not be, these being matters for individual LEAs to decide. This turned out to be an area of misunderstanding and conflict though the intention was that if the framework offered by the Code was strictly followed, with responsibilities emphasised at the school level, a hierarchy of stages and needs could be established, providing the necessary documentation and evidence forming part of the criteria. The revised 2001 Code has not gone further, though the DfES commissioned specific work in this area from the University of Newcastle (DfES 2000b). This guidance has not been included in the SEN Toolkit, and is awaited with interest.

The 1994 Code represented best SEN practice at the time of its implementation. It had many resource implications which required careful and effective responses, especially in political and economic climates when resources were so scarce. With local management of schools, the responsibility for deployment of these resources rested with schools and their governing bodies as a substantial number of children experiencing special educational needs were expected to be supported from funds already delegated to them. The 1994 Code reinforces a number of key assumptions and requirements. Three require special mention.

First, 20 per cent of children are considered likely to experience a special educational need at some time in their school career. The majority will be educated in the mainstream, with a very small number (2 per cent) provided with a Statement of Special Educational Needs.

Second, all children experiencing special educational needs, i.e. all of the 20 per cent, will have their needs met. This means specific, targeted resources to support these children, with documentation to provide evidence of the necessary planning, consultation and teaching.

Third, specific staff will undertake responsibility for SEN provision, ranging from the nominated 'responsible person' to the Special Educational Needs Coordinator and special educational needs teams in larger schools.

If, as expected, more children attract support and stay in the mainstream, without a Statement, schools will have to allocate their resources as efficiently as possible, given the increased demands imposed on staff by the Code's new procedures, e.g. IEP meetings, preparation of paperwork, consultation with parents. There is also the challenge of ensuring that suitably qualified and experienced staff are available to implement appropriate learning programmes, in addition to supporting the ordinary class teacher. Consideration will therefore need to be given to in-service training and other requirements of the teaching and non-teaching staff.

The 1994 Code introduced a number of requirements. First, and most importantly, children have a right to make their views known; they should be listened to and be encouraged to participate in decision making; this is strengthened in the 2001 revisions. Special Educational Needs Tribunals also actively seek information on children's perspectives, reinforcing the increasing importance of listening to children (see also UNESCO 1989 on the UN Convention on the Rights of the Child (Jenkins 1993)).

Second, schools were required to maintain a register of all children experiencing special educational needs and publish their Special Educational Needs Policy, detailing the arrangements for the children and the people responsible. The revised Code abandons this requirement in the interests of reducing bureaucracy. Special Educational Needs Coordinators (SENCOs) were expected to ensure that an Individual Education Plan (IEP) is drawn up for all pupils from Stage 2 onwards; the revised Code makes similar expectations though the concept of stages is abandoned in favour of School Action and School Action Plus (see Chapter 6). The requirement for schools to follow a graduated approach in their responses to children's SEN remains. Ofsted inspections are to consider the effectiveness of school policies and practices in the light of the Code.

Third, LEAs are expected to provide parents with the support of a parent partnership officer or Independent Parental Supporter, who can offer advice and information during statutory assessment; such a person should be independent of the LEA. In drawing up Statements of Special Educational Needs, LEAs must detail precisely the needs of the child and the educational requirements, including broad objectives. When disputes arise, parents are to have access to a quick and independent system of appeal at Special Educational Needs Tribunals (but see Chapter 10); these are to be non-departmental public organisations, completely independent of local and central government. LEAs must have regard to the Code; and these Tribunals will be specifically concerned with whether or not they have made the right decision in the particular circumstances. LEAs must draw up a Transition Plan for children who are aged 14 or over to prepare for the transition from school to adult life; this replaces the statutory reassessment (at the age of 13½ to 14½) under previous legislation.

All of these, except for the requirement of an SEN register, apply under the revised Code. Chapter 2 provides the context within which the revisions were made to the 2001 Code of Practice and details the key changes. It deals with the fundamental principles which continue to underpin and inform the revised Code, including its aims and objectives.

2 The revised Code of Practice: context and key changes

The 2001 revised Code of Practice was written in the context of the Labour Government's Special Educational Needs Action Programme entitled *Excellence in Schools* (DfEE 1997). This emphasised the need to reduce bureaucracy in response to school concerns about teacher workloads and the effect on morale. It was also aimed at maintaining the focus on raising standards within a climate of accountability and best value. With increasing delegation and fair funding, schools were being expected to show returns in pupil performance, especially at respective key stages and at GCSE.

There was also concern that too many LEAs had percentages of Statements in excess of the expected 2 per cent average. The costs were considered excessive and the liabilities enormous to the extent that there was need for a revived drive to force down the percentages of Statements in LEAs. Since coming to power, the Labour Government had confirmed its commitment to inclusion; however, this came to be perceived more as rhetoric when its White Paper (DfEE 1997) acknowledged the role and continuing existence of special schools. Its inclusive schools' guidance was, however, surprising in its tone and focus when the rights to mainstream education were strongly emphasised. Having completed legislation on the Human Rights Act 1998 and the 2001 SEN and Disability Discrimination in Education Acts, it had to reconcile many issues so that it was inevitable that rights would be strengthened in as many areas as possible and discrimination more strongly dealt with. The revised Code had to show cognisance of all these issues while at the same time needing to remain a manageable document. That it succeeded to provide a balanced perspective, albeit within a rather restricted framework constrained by existing legislation, is a credit to its authors.

The revised Code recognised the need for slimmer documentation and for a family of documents to inform special educational needs practice. The changes in emphasis were to be those of increased action at school level, placing responsibilities on schools themselves within the government's agendas for continuing school improvement, and raising standards. Increased pupil participation was also expected within the human rights and children's rights agenda. Concerns about rising tribunal appeals also needed to be addressed, and improved parent partnership and conciliation services were expected.

The timetable for consultation was spread over two years. This started in July 2000 and, although publication was initially planned in the Spring term of 2001, the new Code did not appear until November 2001, coming into force in January 2002. Its status remains that of guidance though, as has been demonstrated already by its predecessor, it will exercise considerable force in the law courts, influencing and shaping case law, e.g. the Somerset judgment.

Key changes

The revised Code retains the key principles and beliefs detailed in the original. The key changes are as follows.

- Schools are no longer required to maintain an SEN register. While this register is recognised as serving a useful purpose, the administrative workload is considered to be a burden to be abandoned if bureaucracy is to be reduced. Where teachers wish to continue with this practice, there is nothing to stop them doing so but abandoning the requirement means that they may also no longer fear the prospect of litigation in this respect if the challenge should ever arise. They must, however, tell parents whenever they make provision for a child they consider to be experiencing special educational needs.

- Schools can continue to make requests for statutory assessent. However, this now has the same status as a parental request, the reasoning being that schools are deemed to act in loco parentis. Research, e.g. Hayden 1997, Marsh 1998, Allan 1999 and Ballard 1999, shows that schools are often acting to serve their own needs and not necessarily furthering the interests of parents or children. Indeed, many parents feel disempowered by them (Allan 1999, Ballard 1999). However, under the revised Code, parents have the right of appeal to an SEN tribunal following a school's request for statutory assessment. The time limit of six weeks for decision making by the LEA also applies.

- The role and status of the SENCO is further recognised. The time required for discharging their duties is also clarified though falling short of this being specified (see also Bowers *et al.* 1998). Their sources of funding are also clarified; these are intended to be from schools' core or base budget which carries an element for special educational needs. It is not intended to be from SEN allocations for specific children; nor is it meant to be from allocations to schools from LEAs' SEN Audits. Most schools are expected to fund the salaries of SENCOs from their Additional Educational Needs Allocations (AEN), which may be as much as 20 per cent of their core budgets.

- Guidance is available for a range of educational settings from early years through to primary and secondary schools. While much of this information is repeated as being applicable to all settings, colour coding makes reference easier. Differences recognise those that apply due to contextual settings, e.g. in early years settings and secondary schools. The consistent theme, however, is about 'school action', emphasising the roles and responsibilities of education providers to add value to the process of teaching and learning.

Previous stages applicable under the original Code of Practice are replaced by 'School Action' and 'School Action Plus'. 'School Action' refers to the old Stages 1 to 3, i.e. school-based stages, while 'School Action Plus' refers to assessment, planning and provision that involves external agencies and is over and above what the school can do on its own.

- Schools are referred to the National Curriculum Inclusion Statement and to the new Ofsted framework for the inspection of inclusive practice (see also QCA 1999, 2000). Pupil participation is confirmed to be a goal for all learners. Their active participation in such processes as assessments, target setting, IEPs, progress and Annual Reviews is not only encouraged but expected.

- Pupils' special educational needs are to be recognised and not cause discrimination in any way; schools should be able to demonstate that no child has been less favourably treated on the grounds that they may experience special educational needs. They should also be able to admit the majority of children. Refusing to do so will be more difficult to justify as schools will need to explore all reasonable steps to include children; the expectation is that it should be very rare indeed for such steps to be exhausted and for the admission of children experiencing special educational needs to be argued to interfere with the efficient education of other children or to be an inefficient use of resources. There is an increased potential for litigation on grounds of discrimination on the basis of special educational needs.

- Guidance is provided for the admission arrangements in units and classes of 30 children in Key Stage 1; exceptions apply for children with Statements of Special Educational Needs in the year of admission.

- The concept of 'additional to or otherwise different from resources normally available in schools' is reinforced and extended. This same principle is applied to IEPs and is indeed consistent with the whole of the revised Code. IEPs are expected to provide information 'additional to or otherwise different from' planning for ordinary pupils, e.g. in terms of attainments, target setting, provision or review processes. IEPs are also expected to be crisp, short and user friendly with three to four objectives. This re-emphasises the need for IEPs to list realistic and attainable objectives as opposed to overfull descriptive documents that did little to further children's progress. IEPs are now given a timescale for reviews; twice a year is recommended within reviews which should avoid undue formality. Group IEPs are also introduced; these are particularly appropriate in special schools or classes with a number of pupils who may be experiencing similar difficulties in learning and therefore require similar planning and targets.

- LEAs are expected to treat school requests for statutory assessment in the same way that they would respond to a parental request, i.e. within six weeks. They are expected to avoid bureaucracy and not to ask for extra paperwork from schools, building on the good practice in some LEAs which treat information contained in the statutory assessment request as educational advice if this is agreed.

- There is a requirement for the LEA to specify or quantify provision in Part 3 though some flexibility is allowed in appropriate cases. The LEA can describe a type of school in Part 4 without naming a specific school. It is also required to reduce the number of Statements, maintaining them only when necessary. LEAs are encouraged to clarify and confirm their criteria for ceasing to maintain Statements.

- Schools and LEAs are required to plan the transfer of children at each key stage of education. This is to be carried out at the review meeting prior to the final year in the child's current school.

- LEAs are expected to amend all Statements by 15 February prior to the child's transfer in September of that same year. Schools no longer have to send copies of Annual Reviews to a wide range of parties; parents and those who attended or are deemed to have a key involvement and continuing interest should receive copies.

- There is increased emphasis on Parent Partnership and LEAs are expected to provide an independent conciliation element, e.g. from a voluntary provider, the test being that this must be independent of the LEA.

The new Code could have been a Code of conciliation in an age where education is becoming more and more contentious and subject to increasing litigation. Since the House of Lords' ruling on educational negligence, i.e. that education practitioners have the same duty of care to their clients as those in other professions, it seems increasingly likely that compensation claims against LEAs will rise, leading to inceased expenditure in legal and compensation costs where awarded, as opposed to the required investments in education (see Harris 1997). Millions are already being spent on SEN tribunals to deal with disagreements and conflicts (e.g. see SEN Tribunal, 1999/2000); more will be required to deal with claims of disability discrimination with the setting up of Special Educational Needs and Disability Discrimination Tribunals (SENDIST). While this bodes well for human and disability rights, it is regrettable that legislation has been deemed necessary to secure them. It is also a concern that more litigation must mean less resources for schools and ultimately less for children experiencing difficulties in learning. This very dilemma of differentiating at the individual level while at the same time promoting the collective good lies at the heart of the problem in education, one that could have been better addressed by the revised Code (see Chapter 10). There is not enough said in the Code about the needs of the whole school and of other children; the emphasis is on individual approaches and the individual child, derived from outmoded concepts of needs and disabilities. Granted that legislation requires such an emphasis, there is no reason to prevent new legislation being passed to repeal outmoded education thinking. The move towards more inclusive schooling has been made by amending section 316 of the 1996 Education Act in the 2001 SEN and Disability In Education Act; could other areas have been similarly addressed? What if the Code placed the needs of the individual in the context of classrooms and the needs of other children? The revised Code was intended to fit within the government's agenda to reduce bureaucracy (DfEE 1997); it succeeds in making only cosmetic changes. Opportunities to reduce teacher workloads and bureaucracy within LEAs have been largely missed. On the positive side, IEP and Annual Review requirements have been simplified;

however, the demand for Statements, for a long time recognised as the time bomb for SEN, is unlikely to be reduced. Providing a right of appeal to parents in respect of schools' requests for statutory assessment will increase bureaucracy in LEAs, reinforce schools' pursuits of Statements as a means of increasing their limited SEN resources (Marsh 1998) and perhaps even compound conflicts resulting in arbitration at SEN tribunals. Where does a school stand in relation to parental appeals at SEN tribunals when these derive from its own request for statutory assessment refused by the LEA? Are schools part of the LEA or are they separate and distinct entities whose conduct is only regulated by legislation, e.g. the Schools Framework Act 1998 and the Code of Practice for Schools (DfES 2001)? There seems to be so much legislation to regulate proceedings rather than addressing some problems at source. No doubt this may be proving necessary given the lobbying of pressure groups (see Gross 1996, Bowers 1998) and government's drive to reduce the power and influence of LEAs; legislation then becomes the surest way of retaining a degree of control, albeit centralised.

LEAs have been expected to reduce the percentage of Statements issued and the Code was meant to assist with this task. I think it will fail to do so, fuelling both more demand and conflict. The government should decide whether it wants more Statements in circulation or not. It should not both promote more demand and expect LEAs to control and manage this while more resources are being devolved to schools. Why is it that the percentage of Statements maintained by an LEA is a public performance indicator expected to reduce annually while other pressures are added to exert the opposite force? There is no logic in this; neither is there any reason to believe that increased conciliation and mediation now expected of LEAs will reduce the conflicts likely to arise from increased routes of appeal to the SEN tribunal. To an outsider, it may look as if various interests within government itself are not aligned to a shared stategy; there are far too many deviations, tensions and conflicts which are somehow left to legislative bodies to resolve. Parents and schools can expect more SEN resources; more tribunals are accepted as a norm, with all the resources this will require. LEAs are expected to have lesser roles and influences; they are intended to become more passive and less directive but only up to a point and that is reached when accountabilities are challenged. Whether these may have been caused by them or not is then immaterial as they retain accountabilities for third parties within their jurisdiction, notably schools.

The beginning of this millennium is likely to be remembered as an age when education moved on from being medicalised; at long last, it has managed to rid itself of the shackles of the medical deficit model. However, it is being increasingly legalised and traumatised to the extent of facing increasing legislation and concurrent litigation. This is a tragedy: the death of education as it used to be and the start of a new era, one where teachers are increasingly needing to be cautious and to stifle their creativity in order to avoid the risks of litigation.

The premise on which this handbook is based is that any complex activity requires sound planning, purposeful action, careful monitoring through systematic records and objective evaluation. The Code emphasises this need in teaching and calls for a cycle of planning, assessment and review. This is the minimum requirement, especially with children whose learning needs are severe and complex, requiring a rigorous approach in the education they receive. In these cases, the task of responding effectively to the children's needs calls for an understanding of what these needs are, and systematic planning as to the necessary teaching and action. This is followed by evaluation of any intervention or programme used. Such an approach focuses on the actions and creativity of the teacher, without involving the need to attribute learning responses and/or failures to factors 'within the child'. Thus, there is no blame attached to the child's innate ability, disposition or other circumstances, the responsibility being very much on the parent or teacher whose task is to take account of all relevant factors that may be having an effect on learning and to include these in their intervention. However, there now lurks the 'duty of care' that every teacher must exercise; i.e. they must apply the most up-to-date, relevant and knowledgeable approaches expected of an average competent teacher (Harris 1997).

This handbook does not propose to cover the requirements of the Code in detail as this is best done by reading the Code itself. Instead, what follows is a translation of some of the key requirements into practical guidance for teachers and others. The focus is on what the Code means to parents, teachers, governors and other staff with direct responsibility for children's learning. This includes discussions of the kind of expectations which can be reasonably made and the procedures to be followed in order to 'have regard to the Code' and fulfil its requirements. Guidelines on how to prepare Individual Education Plans (IEPs) are included, together with some suggested proformas. There is also a chapter on how to prepare for meetings, particularly those dealing with Annual Reviews and the preparation of the Transition Plan at post-14 years of age.

Fundamental principles of the revised Code of Practice

The revised Code continues to be firmly based on principles which are intended to influence and guide planning and action in providing for children experiencing special educational needs.

The most significant relates to a child's right to an education in the mainstream; this has been deliberately strengthened to take account of forces towards inclusion. There is a new duty for LEAs to show that they have taken every reasonable step to facilitate inclusion; indeed, the expectation is that very few children will require to be placed outside of mainstream settings (*SEN Toolkit*, DfES 2001).

Entitlement to a broad and balanced curriculum, including the National Curriculum, is reinforced; this addresses the problem previously uncovered by research in the teaching of children experiencing SEN, many of whom have been provided with diluted, unchallenging curricula, on predetermined bases of low abilities or intellect (Dunn 1968). The entitlement of *all* children experiencing difficulties in learning to have their needs addressed, including a recognition of the continuum of needs to be matched with a continuum of provision, is also consolidated.

The rights of pre-schoolers experiencing special educational needs and the need for early and effective intervention are recognised, as is the importance of making provision in early years centres supported and overseen by area SENCOs. Active partnership within and between agencies, with the close involvement of parents, is encouraged. Accountability, efficiency and effectiveness are expected at all stages.

The aims of the 2001 Code of Practice

The aims of the 2001 Code are to help schools and other responsible agencies make effective decisions on how to fulfil their responsibilities with regard to children experiencing special educational needs. It aims to secure best value from SEN resources and to ensure the matching of provision to need through a model of assessment which places the emphasis on 'school action'. It encourages improved practice in schools and in the classroom by ensuring early screening, identification and reporting of learning difficulties, and thorough and progressively more detailed assessments, including prompt planning and intervention. It advocates the keeping of clear and systematic records to enable the monitoring and evaluation of a child's progress. These may be used at information-giving, planning and decision-making meetings, e.g. informal meetings with parents, agreeing IEPs, Annual Reviews, Transition Plan meetings. It suggests that key responsibilities should be identified and allocated to promote effective SEN practice and that parents and teachers should be supported to improve their best endeavours with children.

Children, on the other hand, should be given a voice by requiring that they and their parents are consulted in decision making, whenever possible and appropriate. Their views, alongside those of their parents, should be recorded in statutory and other documentation. LEAs, Health and Social Services should make themselves more accountable to parents by ensuring that statutory assessments are completed on time and within specified limits. Special Educational Needs Tribunals have been set up to resolve disputes and LEAs should ensure that independent conciliation services exist to reduce the need for Tribunal arbitration.

Conclusion

There are significant implications arising from the 2001 Code relating to everybody actively engaged in supporting children experiencing special educational needs. While the Code does not have the full force of law, all parties are required, under the 2001 Education Act, 'to have regard' to its provisions. There are many procedures to think about and processes to be gone through. These range from the planning of IEPs to the conduct of Annual Reviews and the preparation of Transition Plans.

The main objective, however, is to ensure that *all* children receive the most efficient education possible. This implies a degree of accountability in teachers and other professionals whose contribution may be evaluated against the Code's provisions with regard to best practice.

3 Implications for the class teacher

Definition of special educational needs

The Code adopts the definition of special educational needs as laid down in the 1981 Education Act and subsequently in the 1993, 1996 and 2001 Education Acts.

A child has special educational needs if he or she has a learning difficulty which calls for special educational provision to be made for him or her.

A child has a learning difficulty if he or she:
(a) has a significantly greater difficulty in learning than the majority of children of the same age
(b) has a disability which either prevents or hinders the child from making use of educational facilities of a kind provided for children of the same age in schools within the area of the local educational authority
(c) is under five and falls within the definition at (a) or (b) above or would do if special educational provision was not made for the child.

A child must not be regarded as having a learning difficulty solely because the language or form of language of the home is different from the language in which he or she is or will be taught.

Special educational provision means:
(a) for a child over two, educational provision which is additional to, or otherwise different from, the educational provision made generally for children of the child's age in maintained schools, other than special schools, in the area
(b) for a child under two, educational provision of any kind.

(1993 Education Act, Section 156; 1996 Education Act, Section 312)
Source: 1994 and 2001 Codes of Practice, HMSO

Implications for teachers and schools

The concept of special educational needs appears to be conditional on the existence of a learning difficulty which is defined in (a) to (c) above. These defini-

16

tions have direct implications for teachers and other education providers, impinging directly on accepted practice and beliefs. The notion that children 'have' learning difficulties is increasingly questioned in the literature as these are not distinct traits or entities located within children; difficulties in learning arise from children's interactions and experiences within schools (see, for instance, Potts et al. 1995, Ramjhun 2001). Discourses about children experiencing difficulties in learning are more appropriate as these can encompass the role of other factors. The problematic concept of SEN has already been highlighted and its enshrinement in law gives it more credibility and validity than it deserves. How can children have SEN? How does it feel to have SEN? Are SEN really those of children or the needs of other parties? (see Galloway *et al.* 1994 for further discussion). Bearing these concerns in mind, we can now explore each of the issues raised in the legal definition of SEN in turn.

(a) A child has a learning difficulty if he or she has a significantly greater difficulty in learning than the majority of children of the same age

The words 'significantly greater difficulty in learning' are of the essence here. How this is arrived at in practice is certainly subject to individual variation, though it is likely to be interpreted as performance which falls below the bottom 2 per cent of the child's age group.

Teachers might compare the child's performance on such measures as in the following sections 1 to 5.

1. *National Curriculum Attainments* – especially the discrepancy between the achievements of the 'average' child in a particular year group and those of the child experiencing special educational needs.

Teachers could prepare a list of the attainments of children in their class and make a simple frequency count, i.e. how many are achieving at each level of the National Curriculum. For example, out of a group of 50 11-year-olds, there may be 25 achieving at Level 3, 15 working towards Level 3 and 10 still working towards Level 2, one of whom is working within Level 1. Changing these figures into percentages would lead to the following:

Percentage	National Curriculum Level
50	Level 3
30	Towards Level 3
18	Towards Level 2
2	Within Level 1

Frequency counts can be maintained for individual classes and year groups and aggregated to provide percentages for the whole school. These provide norms, the idea being that the bottom 20 per cent and especially the 2 per cent will attract funding from the school's special educational needs budget to provide the help required. Children in the 20 per cent can be followed up and appropriately supported. Those in the bottom 2 per cent can then be considered for intensive support and, if need be, for recommendation to the LEA for statutory assessment if additional funding is required. The LEA would no doubt wish to see evidence of effective and purposeful intervention over a period of time.

In the above example, the average 11-year-old is achieving at Level 3, i.e. the standard reached by 50 per cent of the children in that year group. Eighty per cent are achieving or working towards Level 3, with only 20 per cent working towards Level 2. Out of this 20 per cent, 2 per cent are *significantly underachieving*.

2. *Results of reading, spelling or number assessments* – perhaps centiles from reading/spelling ages.

Standardised tests are useful in that they provide norms in relation to reading/spelling ages. However, these should be used cautiously and interpreted in context. Teachers should also incorporate their own assessments from their knowledge of the child, e.g. his style of learning and progress over time. The latter information is very useful and pertinent, making up for deficiencies which are intrinsic to standardised assessments. For example, children may score at very low levels in a standardised reading or spelling assessment which is focusing on accuracy but may be developing the necessary phonic or other word attack skills they are being taught. These are more relevant to teaching and the child's needs and normally such discrepancies should cause no surprise or concern to parents and others if the value and reliability of standard assessments are in question. Similarly, many children are able to read fluently but with little understanding of meaning, thereby masking their difficulties.

3. *Profiles of achievement in different areas of the curriculum* – Forming a profile of the child's achievements is an extremely useful process. This normally serves to indicate the child's abilities and needs, highlighting problem areas as well as those which could be used to boost the child's confidence and self-esteem. Psychologists often find that a child who was initially thought to be of low ability because of low academic attainments may be functioning at average levels or more. However, they fail to achieve in a particular area, which depresses their overall attainments and makes them appear to be less able than they are. This is the case with children who experience a specific learning difficulty, perhaps in reading and/or spelling. Their work may show significant weaknesses and they may also be experiencing difficulties with access to the literacy components of the curriculum. In these cases, it is useful to draw up a profile which shows the child's cognitive strengths and weaknesses. This helps with planning, such as which area to address within teaching, the kinds of material and approaches which are more likely to ensure effective access to the curriculum, and the teaching of compensatory strategies.

4. *The child's behaviour and learning* – It is a truism that a happy, well settled child is able to devote more time and energy to his learning compared with one with a variety of worries and anxieties, not all immediate or obvious. Consequently, teachers should be alert to signs of children not applying themselves, seeming unable to concentrate or to persevere with tasks. A measure of their concentration span or work output is often helpful as are observations focusing on interactions with peers, teachers and other adults. Other useful indices relate to:

Communication patterns – Does the child show a desire to communicate? Or does he avoid or resist encouragement to do so? Does the child maintain or avoid eye contact? Does he take turns or are communications one way?

Communication contents – maturity of language, repetition of words, ideas, extent of vocabulary, information content, sentence construction, clarity of speech sounds.

Level of understanding – including development of listening skills.

Personal skills – relating to self help and independence, e.g. dressing, eating, washing, toileting.

Personal safety – road sense, conformity to norms and conventions, e.g. not climbing/sitting on window sills or jumping out of windows, not wandering or going with strangers.

Physical needs – mobility, sight, hearing, gross and fine motor skills.

5. *Other factors relevant to the child's learning* – The majority of children are in caring, supportive families, concerned for their welfare, happiness, development and education. Others may not be so fortunate (see Rutter and Madge 1981, Utting 1997). It is therefore crucial that teachers are aware of and take into account the child's individual circumstances, particularly the level of help and support available from the immediate family, parents or carers. The facilities for study and self-development which families can or cannot afford are other important considerations. Any experience of care or change of care outside of the immediate family, including any future change pending, also needs to be taken into account. Any event or incident which is likely to have a significant impact on the child, e.g. a bereavement, experience of abuse or the diagnosis of a critical illness in the child or other members of the family, separation of the parents or divorce, is also likely to cause tensions and affect the child's emotional readiness for learning.

(b) A disability which either prevents or hinders the child from making use of educational facilities of a kind provided for children of the same age in schools within the area of the local education authority.

This could mean a physical or sensory disability, e.g. lack of mobility, hearing or visual impairment, but could also include other difficulties such as an emotional or social difficulty which makes it impossible for the child to work cooperatively with his teachers or his peers. It could also be a combination of needs which require provision different from or exceeding those normally provided in schools, e.g. a profoundly disabled child experiencing physical, sensory and severe learning difficulties. However, LEAs are changing the way in which schools are resourced so that it is becoming increasingly possible for children experiencing the most complex difficulties to receive help in the mainstream; for example, Southampton LEA provides outreach services from special schools in order to promote inclusion (SCC 1998, 1999, Ramjhun 2001). The revised Code will encourage such initiatives, especially as it is no longer acceptable to argue that children's needs cannot be met in mainstream education, the test having moved on to demonstrating that every reasonable step has been tried and that the child's education will interfere with the education of other children or will constitute an inefficient use of resources (DfEE 2001b).

(c) Child is under five and falls within the definition at (a) or (b) above or would do if special educational provision was not made for the child

This relates to pre-school children who have needs as described in (a) and (b) above, which require early and structured intervention. This could be provided, of course, in a nursery, language or other units, or even in nursery classes of infant schools where these are established.

Children whose home language is different from the language of instruction
The Code repeats previous advice that a child must not be regarded as experiencing a learning difficulty on the sole basis that their language is different from the language of instruction in school. Bilingualism is an asset and should be recognised as such.

There is therefore a particular need for caution in the type of assessments to be used with these children, especially for these to be culture free and culture fair as far as is possible. They should also include results relating to performance which are not directly influenced or affected by lack of English, e.g. non-verbal tests.

Implications for the class teacher

The Code makes significant requirements on all teachers, irrespective of whether or not they have responsibility for special educational needs. All teachers are, of course, teachers of children with special educational needs and in a sense it is true to say that when a child has these needs so does the teacher. This is because of the special care and planning required to ensure that learning progresses.

The Code formalises the planning process. Though teachers have always prepared and maintained records, this is now a requirement in the form of the Individual Education Plan. Therefore, irrespective of the action required by the child under the Code's procedures, all class teachers are required to have regard to the provision the child requires and they may need to adjust their practice to meet the requirements. There is no difference either at the pre- or post-statutory stage, except that the child with more significant needs is likely to require more detailed planning and responses. The implications for the teacher at each stage are outlined below but there should be no assumption that the processes are separate and distinct, only that the requirements at the post-statutory stage are likely to be higher. In an age where education negligence claims may increase, records are likely to represent important documentation for the courts; as Harris (1997) says, without such records judges might be persuaded to accept the argument put forward by litigants that the facts as presented speak for themselves.

Pre-statutory stage

The class teacher needs to demonstrate that all the required action has been taken, with appropriate documentation completed over a period of time.

Parents should have been consulted at an early stage and regular communication maintained with them. A number of strategies should have been tried to address the child's SEN, carefully planned and under the close supervision of the teacher, including consultation with the Special Educational Needs Coordinator.

This means setting clear objectives, monitoring progress on a regular basis and consulting, if in doubt, normally with the Special Educational Needs Coordinator. Objectives and progress should be reviewed and new targets set. Teachers should work within specified and agreed time frames and ensure that Individual Education Plans are being implemented.

Post-statutory stage

Class teachers need to demonstrate that they are fully conversant with the contents and requirements of the Statement and that they are working to the requirements through clearly stated objectives within planned and systematic programmes. They should, of course, also be able to show that they have been as diligent as they were during the 'pre-statutory stage'. They must, in addition, plan and contribute to the Annual Review, provide accurate and detailed information as and when required. They should be able to answer questions from parents and other parties and be able to produce the evidence on the rare occasions when challenged. Defending a particular approach or point of view at a Special Educational Needs Tribunal may be necessary.

Action for teachers

1. Make sure parents know what you are doing, rather than just your concerns.
2. Enlist their help and make it clear that you wish to work in partnership with them, sharing responsibility for the task of helping their child.
3. Consult with your Special Educational Needs Coordinator and keep them in touch with the work that you are doing.
4. Keep full and clear records.
5. Do not show any unease, and speak with confidence, at meetings and Annual Reviews, armed with the facts about the child's learning. Remember that you are the only person with direct and daily contact with the child and therefore know as much as and probably more than anyone else.
6. Come to meetings prepared, with all the necessary records and programmes. You are likely to be asked about
   - National Curriculum Attainments (and their meanings to parents)
   - reading/spelling/writing attainments
   - number skills
   - factors affecting learning in the classroom
   - whether targets agreed in the IEPs are being met; if not, whether they are being systematically addressed.

7. Show that you have planned and made arrangements to enhance learning in the classroom (crucial for all children, including the child experiencing special needs).
8. Know about, accumulate and use the appropriate material with children who experience difficulties in learning. This is one of the areas in which your Special Educational Needs Coordinator is a useful resource.
9. Discuss problems and concerns early and keep everybody informed, not forgetting your head teacher and Special Educational Needs Coordinator.
10. Set yourself objectives which are SMART:
    S – Simple
    M – Measurable
    A – Achievable
    R – Realistic
    T – Timely and translatable into teaching terms
11. Discuss and agree your objectives with children; involve them in the process. Teaching is not an activity directed at children; it is to be undertaken with them so that the teaching and learning experience is productive and fulfilling for all parties. Your targets are the children's targets too; they must know what is expected of them.
12. Follow the cycle of:

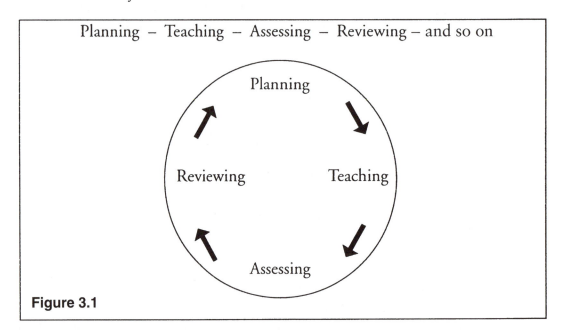

Planning – Teaching – Assessing – Reviewing – and so on

Planning

Reviewing   Teaching

Assessing

Figure 3.1

Implementation of the Code of Practice in secondary schools

Secondary schools offer a context which is different and organisationally more complex to that existing in primary schools. There are more staff, tighter timetabling constraints, more complex curricular and organisational arrangements, which all have to be taken account of in planning for the child experiencing difficulties in learning (see also Bowers *et al.* 1998). Ordinarily, a great deal of the organising and responsibility falls on the Special Educational Needs Coordinator and most schools have special needs departments which serve as bases and points of reference for children, parents and staff alike.

The difference between primary and secondary schooling is that the child in the secondary school is taught by many more teachers, as opposed to just the one or the very few they were used to before. The former tend to be subject specialists and may not be able to see or teach the child for more than a few lessons per week. This normally means that they need longer to get to know the child, and are perhaps able to form impressions about performance in their subject area but without a complete view of the whole child in his functioning. Consultation and cooperation within and between subject areas is, therefore, likely to produce dividends, as it is interesting to see how the child is working in areas different to one's own. This may at minimum mean no more than comparing notes or reading subject reports on a child who is causing concern, though cooperative planning and active collaboration will be necessary for more severe problems, e.g. the child who is disruptive in lessons or who is truanting.

The action required at School Action and School Action Plus of the Code of Practice apply to the secondary schoolteacher in the same way as they do in primary schools. However, there are some essential differences.

Roles and responsibilities of subject teachers

Early forms of School Action may show a variety and range of responses from subject specialists which then need to be organised to form an overview of the child. Subject teachers' responsibilities are to provide a clear picture of how the child is functioning in their class and in particular how he is dealing and coping with the requirements of the curriculum. They should give an indication of the child's attitude, interest, disposition and application to learning in their particular subject area. They should also comment on the child's performance and how this compares with that of his peers and what would normally be expected. An indication of the arrangements that are having to be made to accommodate the child's difficulties is necessary.

Such information need not be too detailed at the initial stages of supporting children at School Action as the purpose is to collate and compare teachers' views and observations of children causing concern, with a view to clarifying the nature of that concern and the action necessary.

Later stages or steps within School Action of the Code represent a different matter, especially when in spite of purposeful action progress is not forthcoming. This is when the Special Educational Needs Coordinator takes the lead and he/she will wish to be advised of the specific subject areas which continue to cause concern and how the relevant staff propose to provide the additional help required. The needs of subject staff, in terms of teaching techniques, materials and resources, including the support arrangements to be made either within or outside of the classroom, will have to be agreed, including their timetabling implications especially if 'withdrawal teaching' is deemed necessary. Repeating lessons missed due to timetabling problems will require planning, and information will be required on differentiation in the subject areas causing concern.

At the very minimum, such differentiation has to ensure that the child is able to comprehend and deal effectively with the requirements of the curriculum, with a degree of success. Differentiation must not be confused with a dilution of the curriculum where a child is expected to do less or is only able to complete a task with help. Teachers should therefore ensure that differentiation is both by task and by outcome. Records will help show where progress is being made and will be essential in subject areas of concern.

From such stages onwards, the process of coordination assumes greater significance and if this is to proceed smoothly a contact person or point of reference is required for all parties and particularly for the child and his parents. This needs to be agreed quite early on and is normally the child's tutor at the earlier stage and the Special Educational Needs Coordinator from later stages onwards, working closely with the year tutor. Information needs to be channelled consistently through these sources, making sure that all the necessary information is readily available to deal with any queries, requirements, proposals or recommendations.

Choosing options in Year 9 (i.e at 14 years of age) represents another critical stage which secondary teachers need to be especially aware of, both leading up to and after the consultation meetings with parents. Parents, and indeed children, will expect to receive clear advice and guidance relating to their performance, fully documented and clearly explained to enable them to make informed decisions as to which options to select. Children at either School Action or School Action Plus of the Code of Practice will need this information, together with advice on how possible difficulties can be tackled when pursuing certain subjects, e.g. literacy requirements in history, maths in geography, in addition to the requisite skills in some subjects, e.g. reasoning and deduction in maths and science, and perceptual and creative skills in drama and art. Strategies to bypass avoidable difficulties with access can also be discussed, e.g. the use of word processing with spellchecks, voice activated dictaphones, taped texts, differentiated worksheets for a child experiencing a specific literacy difficulty or Braille resources for a visually impaired child. Furthermore, supervision and safety requirements in some subjects will need addressing, e.g. safety in science, home economics and physical education.

The preparation of Individual Education Plans is also likely to present different requirements in the secondary school. It will be left to the specialist, the subject teacher, to prepare these. The essential requirement is for learning to take place and to progress at a satisfactory pace. This requires a clear appreciation of the skills, knowledge and understanding necessary at different stages of the child's development, a breakdown of these into manageable components, with clear teaching objectives and timescales for their achievement and a willingness to look beyond one's subject area, e.g. to make allowances for the literacy components of maths worksheets or science. A commitment to collaborate with other subject teachers, including flexibility with teaching style, pace and lesson content, is also helpful.

Finally, the preparation of Transition Plans in Year 9 will require careful planning and coordination within and between subject departments. This replaces the statutory reassessment procedures which used to take place under the terms of the 1981 Education Act. As a requirement of the 1996 Education Act, the importance of ensuring a clear, comprehensive and coherent plan cannot be emphasised too strongly.

The Transition Plan is intended to prepare for children's smooth transition from school, with arrangements made well beforehand to ensure that their future needs and requirements are effectively met. LEAs delegate the preparation of Transition Plans to schools and this is normally carried out at meetings which run in tandem with Year 9 Annual Reviews. The revised Code introduces the Connexions Service to this process; the Connexions Service Personal Adviser has a key role in Transition (see Chapter 9).

Transition Plan – key issues

The key issues regarding preparation of the Transition Plan are:
1. *The child's educational and vocational requirements at post-16 years of age* – This will require information about the curriculum needed; that is, whether or not a full mainstream curriculum is envisaged. The student might be able to follow A level studies or might be better suited to an NVQ course. This would need to be established, including any special requirements to ensure full access to the course – for example, a person without use of the upper limbs who undertakes chemistry or computer studies at A level, or a wheelchair-bound child wishing to attend a college without lifts or facilities for the disabled. Some students might prefer and be more suited to a vocational course; for example, children experiencing moderate learning difficulties or with basic skills deficits. In these cases, courses and their support requirements will need to be identified early; i.e. any special component with which help might be required, for example simple maths for estimation, timekeeping and budgeting.
2. *Staffing and supervision arrangements* – Staffing and training needs should be addressed prior to pupil admission. If specialists are required to continue their involvement, e.g. physiotherapists, audiologists, teachers of the visually impaired, occupational therapists, they would need to be alerted and involved at and beyond the Transition Plan stage. Their advice may also be needed by the post-16 establishment on matters such as the siting and number of ramps, disabled toilets and lifts.
3. *Review arrangements, following preparation of Transition Plan* – On completion of the Transition Plan, there will be some two years before children transfer to the next stage of their education. Therefore, the Plan will require review and updating yearly and this will be the responsibility of the secondary school staff, probably the Special Educational Needs Coordinator, assisted by the relevant teaching and non-teaching staff.

Conclusion

It often appears that when children transfer from primary to secondary schooling, the focus changes from teaching the pupil to teaching the subject. This should not be the case. The emphasis should always be on teaching the learners; only in this way can the detailed knowledge about their needs translate into effective teaching objectives to ensure progress with the curriculum. It is, however, recognised that the performance of secondary schoolteachers is likely to be measured by their pupils' attainments in public examinations. Indeed, the introduction of market forces into education, through the encouragement of competition between schools, open enrolment, parental choice and the publication of league tables, almost makes this a necessity (Potts *et al.* 1995).

The culture of the market-place requires the identification and evaluation of performance indicators which currently emphasise examination attainments. However, other factors are also important, such as the school ethos, its reputation for the good conduct and discipline of its pupils and its arrangements for children experiencing special educational needs (see Ainscow 1991, Skrtic 1991).

4 Implications for schools and governing bodies

Introduction

The Code makes some specific requirements of schools. In addition to the action to be taken in the identification, assessment and provision for children experiencing special educational needs, schools are expected to provide information about their Special Educational Needs Policy. This should detail the particular arrangements which apply relating to the teaching and support of children experiencing special educational needs. It should name the 'responsible person' for special needs, who could be the head teacher, special needs Governor or Special Educational Needs Coordinator. It should also provide evaluation of the success or otherwise of the special educational needs arrangements, this having been a requirement in Governors' reports to parents from August 1995.

Duties and responsibilities of governing bodies

The governing bodies of schools have 'to have regard to the Code'. This implies a clear responsibility to ensure that their thinking, planning and approach to special educational needs reflects best practice as suggested in the Code. When the original Code came into force, schools were given time for its requirements to be fully integrated into their Special Educational Needs Policies. This was to enable them to develop their approaches and policies, acknowledging that their starting points would differ, depending on their degree of readiness and previous track record on special educational needs practice. Seven years later, this features again as a requirement with the expectation that best practice as advocated in both the original and revised Code will be reflected in schools.

The role of the governing body remains as it has been since 1994. This is to influence and support whole-school policies but with the specified duties to formalise and produce the Special Educational Needs Policy; to monitor, support and evaluate implementation of this Policy and to report on its effectiveness to parents in the Governors' annual reports, including any significant changes made to it. Governors have been required to include a summary of the Policy in school prospectuses since 1995. They have also had to identify and name a 'responsible person' who was to be kept informed of children experiencing special educational needs and who had the responsibility to pass this information to other parties who have a role in teaching and supporting children to overcome barriers to their participation in learning.

Governors continue to have duties to identify, make and report on provision for children experiencing special educational needs; ensure provision for their effective inclusion and identify gaps in provision which they can help to remediate. Alternatively, they can collaborate with other schools and governing bodies, or with the LEA, in order to make a strategic response, especially when it would be uneconomic for a particular school to respond on its own, e.g. providing expensive equipment, adjustments or adaptations for a 'rare' type of need, when it would make more sense to provide collectively for such special need. In the original Code, they had to ensure that a register was maintained for children experiencing special educational needs; this requirement has been dropped in order to reduce bureaucracy. However, Governors may still wish to see records maintained of children whose needs are considered to be lifelong, severe and complex. How else would they be able to demonstrate effective professional practice built on sound planning and records in the event of challenge? How would they be able to satisfy their own reporting requirements if the information is not clearly documented? The Code allows them to use crisp, short and succinct documentation as records on which they may make judgements. The aim has been to ensure that the focus is on action and not records for their own sake and this should be one of the criteria governing bodies should use to determine the nature and extent of record keeping. In other words, how do these add value to teaching and learning?

Governing bodies may wish to continue to take the lead strategic role with regard to policy making and leave the operational issues and day to day implementation requirements to named members of staff. In practice, this has meant that policy is formulated by the governing body, in consultation with the head teacher and Special Educational Needs Coordinator. The head teacher undertakes responsibility for its management and implementation and delegates its day to day operation to the Coordinator, or in larger schools to the special needs team. Figure 4.1. shows a possible scenario.

The school's Special Educational Needs Policy

The information to be included in Special Educational Needs Policies was prescribed by Regulations when the original Code was passed (*Special Educational Needs: Information, Regulations*, Regulation 2 and Schedule 1). The main requirements are listed below.

1. *Information about the special education provision available* – This should specify the school's objectives for special educational needs, including details of its admission policy. It should confirm the name of the Special Educational Needs Coordinator and details of any specialist provision, e.g. specialism among the staff, special facilities and units. Information about access for children with dis-

Children experiencing special educational needs: hierarchies and responsibilities

STRATEGY/
POLICY
MAKING

GOVERNING BODY

1. Agrees policy (and budget), bearing in mind need to have regard to the Code

2. Delegates responsibility for implementation of SEN Policy to 'Responsible Person', either:
   Governor for Special Educational Needs
   or
   Headteacher

MANAGEMENT

HEADTEACHER

1. Oversees and reports on implementation of SEN Policy

2. Delegates responsibility for satisfactory operation to SENCO

OPERATION

SEN COORDINATOR

1. Manages day to day operation of policy and reports to headteacher

2. Supports class teachers as and when required

3. Compiles and maintains SEN Records

4. Ensures requirements of the Code are followed and checks that the required documentation is kept and the appropriate action taken

5. Ensures IEPs are drawn up

6. Maintains contact with parents and support services

Figure 4.1 Special Educational Needs Policy: Strategy and Operation

abilities, e.g. adaptations to buildings, lifts, disabled toilets, technological aids, should be included.

2. *Information about the policies for identification, assessment and provision for children experiencing special educational needs* – This should explain how resources are allocated to and among pupils experiencing special educational needs, e.g. whether allocated to individuals or groups, funds from within school resources, top up by the LEA, names and number of support staff, means and frequency of support. It should detail the arrangements for assessing and reviewing pupils' needs, e.g. IEPs, use of assessments within the framework of the National Curriculum, teachers' observational assessments, record keeping, review procedures for IEPs, Annual Reviews. It should also include the arrangements for facilitating access to a broad and balanced curriculum, including the National Curriculum, e.g. differentiation, use of technology for visually impaired children, provision of laptops, dictaphones, use of multi-sensory approaches to teaching, fieldwork facilities.

Approaches to inclusion should be explained, e.g. inclusion in all classes with support, aims and objectives of inclusion schemes, community involvement. Criteria for evaluating success of the Special Educational Needs Policy should also be made explicit, e.g. evidence of improved performance in specified areas, including academic and skills attainments, personal independence, social behaviour, study skills; the contribution and participation of staff and of parents; the whole-school ethos, specialism/success with supporting children experiencing special educational needs. There should be a complaints procedure, e.g. to whom, how, and the process in which the matter is to be dealt with and resolved, including timescales.

3. *Information about the school's staffing policies and partnership with outside agencies* – The policy on special educational needs training should be clearly stated, e.g. in-house, bought in, external courses. So should the support available from outside agencies, e.g. specialist staff from other schools, the LEA, the Health and Social Services. Arrangements for partnership with parents should be detailed, e.g. parents' evenings, Open Door policies, facilities for parents, appointment systems and response times, communication between home and school, home visiting; regularity, intensity and degree of informality in dealings with parents. Links with other schools, colleges, employers should also be described.

Special Educational Needs Policies are expected to provide the framework for schools to use in providing for children experiencing special educational needs. They are intended to be developed by the whole staff, with leadership and support from individuals with the relevant expertise. This is to enable an effective, holistic and cross-curricular approach which focuses on differentiation and provision for the child as the integrating themes. The practicalities of implementation and the necessary support systems and review mechanisms can also be facilitated in this way, leading to a shared approach, agreed and understood by all parties, and therefore not seen to be the sole responsibility of the Special Educational Needs Coordinator.

The Regulations give Policies a quasi-legal status but the active involvement of the governing body, together with the school's senior management, will be of the essence if a policy is to exceed the minimum legal requirements and become a live document for the whole staff to integrate in their practice.

The role of the special educational needs Governor

Special educational needs Governors frequently complain about lack of clarity or specificity with regard to their role. This was one of the findings from a survey carried out by the Advisory Centre for Education (ACE) in 1992/3. Other findings related to the lack of support likely to be available from either the Department for Education (DFE) or from LEAs in the discharge of their statutory duties.

It is crucial that governing bodies are clear from the start as to what is to be reasonably expected of their special educational needs Governor. He or she will need a clear remit detailing the nature and extent of their responsibilities, among the most important of which is the need to be fully conversant with legislation on the education of children experiencing special educational needs. The legislation goes well beyond the Code of Practice and includes the 1996 and 2001 Education Acts, the 1989 Children Act and the 1988 Education Reform Act. SEN Governors should be be aware of and be able to monitor the school's arrangements with regard to the identification, assessment and provision for children experiencing special educational needs. This implies a familiarity with these arrangements through firsthand observation and experience, including close consultation with key members of school staff and parents. They should also be able to represent and act as advocates on behalf of children at meetings with external agencies, including those with the governing body. They must therefore be fully informed about individual children's needs, funding and other school arrangements, and the requirements of staff and governors in respect of training and related special educational needs issues. They act as the main link for parents and others to the governing body. They may convene and chair working parties to influencing the School Development Plan and should be able to report regularly to Governors on their schools' progress in respect of SEN practice.

It is important to note that these responsibilities require the Governor to be a person of suitable experience and ability, able to inspire confidence beyond the governing body. The Advisory Centre for Education (ACE) suggests that the SEN Governor should not be a 'novice appointment', nor necessarily a Governor with a 'particular personal concern about special needs'.

The role of the Special Educational Needs Coordinator

The Code allocates a key responsibility to the Special Educational Needs Coordinator (SENCO) and broke new ground in 1994 by requiring that there should be such a post in every school, with a named person to carry out the role. Their responsibilities are to facilitate the day to day implementation of the school's policy, provide effective liaison, advise and support fellow teachers, and contribute to special educational needs training. They are required to liaise and work in partnership with parents and others within and beyond the LEA, e.g. voluntary and statutory support agencies.

Previously they were required to maintain the school's SEN register but this is no longer a duty; they will nevertheless play key roles in monitoring and overseeing SEN records, e.g. IEPs and Annual Review documentation. Their main role is to coordinate SEN assessment and provision. The literature (e.g. Davies *et al.* 1998, Cowne 2000, Jones *et al.* 2001) suggests that the SENCO has a pivotal role to play in the education of children experiencing SEN, particularly in promoting their inclusion. The revised Code further reinforces this role and acknowledges the range of responsibilities associated with it.

The Coordinator however, is primarily intended to act as a consultant and a resource to fellow teachers. It should not be assumed that they will carry direct responsibility for all children experiencing SEN because of the specific nature and title of their post; this is not practicable or realistic. The responsibility rests with the class or subject teacher, who has the duty to make the provision as planned either in IEPs, the Statement or Annual Review targets and objectives. There are obviously implications for class teachers and Coordinators in terms of time, planning, the availability of learning material and support staff. However, it is not thought that the Code's requirements will depart from existing good practice in schools.

How to formulate and write a Special Educational Needs Policy

1. Agree school's Mission Statement or equivalent at Governors' meeting.
2. Use the Mission Statement to frame the Special Educational Needs Policy.
3. Define the Special Educational Needs Policy in the context of the school's ethos, the needs identified by the governing body and their objectives and aspirations for all children. A statement confirming a commitment to children's rights and their entitlement to a rich and fulfilling curriculum is helpful. Governors should confirm their own values and principles on equality of opportunity and inclusion and how these are to be achieved.
4. Detail in priority order the principal objectives of the Special Educational Needs Policy, the arrangements to support it and particularly the financial and human resource requirements.
5. Provide the names of key staff, including those of the Special Educational Needs Coordinator and the Responsible Person, who are to act as links with parents and outside agencies.
6. Describe how children's learning difficulties are to be identified, the help that will be available and the way in which progress is to be reviewed and evaluated.
7. Include information relating to any specialism which exists among school staff, the existence of special facilities and resources and the availability of external expertise that can be bought in. Any proposed improvement to SEN provision, e.g. additional staffing or increased accessibility, should also be included.

8. Include details of the procedures and processes to be followed in the event of a query or complaint. These should be clearly explained and should provide details of key contacts and the timescale within which responses can be expected. In the event of a complaint, the investigatory procedure that will apply will also require detailing.

9. Describe the consultation and partnership arrangements with parents, the LEA, and other agencies. Schools may helpfully provide details of any local Parent Partnership scheme that is provided by the LEA or of any mediation and conciliation arrangement that they may wish to call upon. In the first instance, parents should of course be addressing their queries to the head teacher, parent governor or chair of the governing body.

10. Include information on how success in achieving the objectives of the Policy is to be evaluated, as well as its form and frequency of reporting.

11. Include a summary of the Policy in the school prospectus.

A photocopiable version of the above is included as a checklist in Appendix 1.

A schools' charter for parents and children?

Most services produce a charter for their service users. This includes education and in many ways the Code of Practice can be interpreted as being a charter for children and parents with regard to SEN services and provision, e.g. IEPs, additional help available and their sources of funding. Schools should be able to demonstrate how children are being helped to overcome barriers to learning and how they are being supported to increase their participation as members of the school community. Parents must be made aware of any concern about their children and if SEN provision is made they must be told about this and the difference this is expected to make.

Governing bodies may wish to consider producing a charter for their schools. With regard to children experiencing special educational needs, this should be a summary of the key issues from the Special Educational Needs Policy, described in no more than two to three pages and detailing the service offered, the progress that can be reasonably expected and the recourse available in the event of dissatisfaction or complaint. Education has come of age in becoming an accountable service. It is no longer just a matter of the professional knowing best or of the classroom being a 'secret garden which neither the politician nor the public can enter' (Galloway *et al.* 1994: 12). It is indeed everyone's business, not least that of children and their parents.

Conclusion

It is crucial that schools are able to produce a balanced and informative Special Educational Needs Policy for circulation to parents. This is the basis of a contract against which the school's intentions, plans and efforts can be evaluated in terms of achievements, shortcomings and outcomes. The Policy, once publicised, is available for use by governors, parents, LEA staff and others to help their understanding of how the school intends to operate in supporting children. It can also be inspected by Ofsted. From this information will be derived a variety of assumptions and expectations; so the more precisely the policy is written the less room there will be for confusion. It is therefore suggested that the Policy be written in a concise, factual manner, preferably with headings and in a style that is clear, jargon free and easily understandable by parents and others.

5 Individual Education Plans

Introduction

Individual Education Plans (IEPs) have been one of the key requirements of the Code since its inception. They have a number of special features, and require the provision of particular information. They replace similar documentation used in the past and are intended to be 'live' documents, to be used in planning, implementation and review of learning programmes. Their format will vary from one authority to another and indeed from school to school. However, the essential requirements are that the IEP should be short and crisp and be directly used to address children's difficulties in learning.

IEPs need not include details of the usual teaching or classroom arrangements that operate for the majority of children. These are more appropriate for lesson plans. The whole purpose of IEPs is to differentiate the requirements of children who experience difficulties in learning in spite of these arrangements. They should therefore, specify the steps being taken which are 'additional to or otherwise different from' those normally operating in classrooms so that the emphasis can be on overcoming barriers to learning. The revised Code emphasises the differentiation required in IEPs to address difficulties in learning and also introduces group IEPs which illustrate an extension of the concept of special educational provision. In law, special educational provision refers to anything that is additional to or otherwise different from the resources normally available in mainstream schools; with IEPs and group IEPs, the focus is on differentiating teaching arrangements. Although it might have been somewhat less confusing to refer to group IEPs as group education plans, they are meant to be for a group of children whose needs are very similar and for whom a differentiated curriculum or teaching approach is appropriate. Group IEPs are particularly appropriate for children in special schools or for those whose curricular needs relate to a specific area, e.g. literacy or numeracy.

IEPs should specify as clearly as possible the nature and extent of the child's learning difficulty, and describe the action to be taken, the intervention programme to be implemented and the special educational provision to be made. They should provide details of the staff to be involved and the frequency of support to be made available and specify the learning programmes and activities to be undertaken and the materials and equipment required. IEPs should set specific targets to be achieved in a given time; there should be no more than three or four targets. These should be SMART – i.e. simple, measurable, achievable, realistic and timely. Success criteria should be included to enable monitoring and evaluation, and planning should involve and empower parents, offering help wherever necessary.

IEPs should include children's views, wishes and perceptions and should involve them in both the planning and implementation. Such pupil participation is not only good practice; it is now an essential requirement in the revised Code. With increasing recognition of children's rights, it was only a matter of time before such a requirement came into force and it is significant that SEN Tribunals now routinely ask for children's views in consideration of any appeal that reaches them.

IEPs may provide brief summaries of any pastoral care or medical requirements so that teachers are able to ensure that these are provided by the relevant agencies. These only need to be specified once and should not require repetition in future IEPs; the information in each IEP should be brief and succinct, with successive IEPs building on the steps taken to address each and every priority identified as requiring action to meet children's SEN. A useful approach is to use IEPs to complement other records, so long as these have purpose and maintain a focus on action.

Similarly, initial IEPs should specify monitoring, assessment and review arrangements, including dates of formal meetings with parents involved. These reviews can maintain the focus on the kind of action schools need to take to enable children's progress. Evidence in the form of agreed performance indicators is helpful.

The functions of the IEP are summarised below. These serve to illustrate the planning, action and review functions that the IEP is intended to serve. These should feature centrally in all IEPs, the most useful ones of which will contain information relating to the targets being set, the success criteria to be used and the outcome achieved, together with details as to the monitoring, staffing and review arrangements.

A good IEP will identify children's current attainments, target specific priority areas of difficulty and show systematic use of diagnostic and assessment techniques in identifying and making provision for difficulties in learning. It will set targets which are directly related to the areas of the learning difficulty and which are specific, measurable and timely. These should be achievable within the timescale set for review and must demonstrate clear appreciation of the issues underpinning the learning difficulties being addressed.

There should be success criteria which relate directly to targets, ensuring that these can be objectively assessed and based on the teacher's knowledge of what can be expected within the timescale specified. Success indicators might focus on frequency of behaviour or skill being taught, the degree of fluency or accuracy achieved (e.g. in reading and spelling) and the rate of learning and speed at which the targeted behaviour or skill is acquired.

Outcome measures can be used to evaluate the success or otherwise of the

A good IEP will:
- identify the child's current attainments
- target specific priority areas of difficulty
- show systematic use of diagnostic and assessment techniques in identifying and making provision for a learning difficulty.

Targets
- set targets which are:
  - directly related to the areas of the learning difficulty
  - specific, measurable, achievable, relevant and teachable within the timescale set for review and in relation to the teacher's knowledge about the pupil.

Success Criteria
- relate success criteria directly to targets, ensuring these can be objectively assessed and based on the teacher's knowledge of what can be expected from the child within the timescale specified
- specify indicators relating to success, e.g. frequency of behaviour/skill being taught, degree/frequency of fluency /accuracy achieved (e.g. in reading/spelling), rate of learning/speed at which skill is acquired.

Outcome
- include outcome measures which can be used to check if targets were:
  - realistic and achievable
  - moving on to the next step of attainment within the priority area.

Provision
- relate provision arrangements to the targets set and specify length and frequency of support.

Monitoring
- include record keeping arrangements and frequency/nature of liaison in the monitoring section.

teaching process and help to determine the next step to be targeted for action. Any priority area being addressed will have a series of these steps and these can be dealt with in an incremental, sequential manner.

IEPs should specify the SEN provision, including the length and frequency of support within an agreed timescale. It may be helpful to number each IEP; this will obviate need for repetition in that later IEPs can be clearly specified as building on previous ones, showing only changes and adjustments made in the light of practice and children's responses. Together IEPs provide useful documentation so that there should be no need for further detailed records of schools' actions in addressing children's SEN. They should provide helpful documentation and evidence in the event of challenges, e.g. at a SEN Tribunal or at judicial review proceedings. Their absence will be difficult to justify in these cases, especially where parents believe their children's difficulties in learning to be long term, severe and complex to the extent of requiring effective responses and a duty of care from schools.

Guidelines for completing an IEP

An Individual Education Plan is meant to be a working document which specifies precisely the action to be taken in order to meet a limited set of learning objectives. This requires a clear appraisal of children's learning difficulties, followed by the setting of realistic and achievable teaching objectives, together with an indication of the resources, material and other facilities that will be required. These are the three essential elements of the IEP which can then be subjected to evaluation and review, within a continuous and systematic planning, teaching and review cycle.

In drawing up an IEP, it is tempting to try to address all of the child's difficulties and attempt to find a solution to all of them. This is a pointless exercise and best avoided. Instead, teachers should identify one or two areas of difficulty which they consider to be the priority for action. This can then be analysed so that a clear picture may be formed on the nature of the learning difficulty. The skills and sub-skills which the child requires to compensate for or overcome the learning difficulty can be broken down to include a baseline as to what the child can and cannot do, using a 'task analysis' approach. A teaching programme can then be planned to focus directly on the needs identified, keeping this specific to the identified priority area. Teaching objectives can be set, taking account of the time frame being worked to; this implies a manageable number of short-term objectives which can be used to demonstrate the progress achieved. Proposals in terms of teaching, counselling or other forms of support needed, e.g. from an assistant, can be kept brief, except for the first IEP when parents may wish to know exactly the provision the school is making. It is more important to specify the material to be used, how this is to be differentiated, the frequency of its use and its applicability to other areas of the curriculum. Teachers should determine how the skill being taught will be consolidated, applied and transferred to all relevant areas and should include success criteria and outcome measures. This will enable feedback and evaluation of the teaching programmes implemented.

Teachers might find the following guidelines helpful when preparing an IEP.

First of all, prepare an IEP for a specific area of learning difficulty, i.e. do not attempt to address the issues of reading, behaviour or other difficulties all at once. Second, beware of falling into the trap of selecting a generalised difficulty as the priority area of focus. If there is evidence of a difficulty that affects all areas of learning, e.g. lack of motivation, distractibility, or lack of application to school work, try to identify the root causes and see if these can be broken down into manageable tasks for remediation. For example, lack of motivation could be the direct result of failure to achieve in learning, perhaps due to a lack of reading skills making the curriculum inaccessible. The child then develops this as a coping strategy to maintain self-esteem and the key task for the teacher is to address the development of literacy as the priority.

It is assumed that an IEP will have a section on the nature of the difficulty; the action to be taken; the support provided and the arrangements for review. Each will now be discussed in turn, with suggested guidelines on their completion.

The nature of the difficulty

There is no need to write at great length when completing this section. Bullet points can be used, as shown below for a child who has literacy difficulties and for whom an IEP is being drawn up. This focuses on remediation of reading difficulties. The focus is on reading only, though the child is known to have other problems. Listing too many of these makes the IEP process unmanageable.

- *John, aged 8, has a sight vocabulary of ten words, as assessed on a 100 key word list.*
- *He recognises letter sounds, with the exception of vowels.*
- *He has a reading age of below six years, as assessed on the British Ability Scales Word Reading Test.*

If possible, include within this section information about what the child can do. This helps with planning. The example concerning John shows some of the tasks possible, e.g. teaching of vowel sounds, increase in sight vocabulary, curriculum implications for an eight-year-old who is not reading at the level required.

The action to be taken

Teaching targets: Include in this section the teaching targets. These should be short term so that they may be reviewed within the IEP period. For John, the teaching targets might be to increase sight vocabulary to 15 words within six weeks and to 20 words or to teach vowel sounds and ensure mastery within a term. It will be necessary to provide material that has been differentiated, taking account of John's low reading ability, and it is also worth considering how to enable John to have access to reading material at his interest level, e.g. by reading to him for a short period every day from a book of his choice. A 'shared reading' approach (see Topping and Wolfendale 1985) may sometimes be helpful, particularly as this can involve and include parents in helping their child to enjoy a reading activity together.

Material, resources, approaches to be used: Include here any special material the child will require. Books on tape, use of language master cards, word books all come to mind for a child experiencing a reading difficulty. Approaches, on the other hand, might include the development of phonics or word attack skills or the use of multi-sensory approaches to reading. If the approach is well known there should not be a requirement for a great deal of detail here, as further information can be found from other sources.

Success criteria: Teachers sometimes find it confusing to differentiate between a teaching target and success criteria. Essentially, the teaching target represents the goal set by the teacher, i.e. what the teacher intends to achieve. Success criteria, on the other hand, provide the measure which the teacher decides will be acceptable at various stages in aiming for the complete achievement of the teaching targets. They help to show the extent to which the targets are being achieved and for what proportion of the time. For example, if the target is to increase sight vocabulary to 20 words within 12 weeks, the success criteria might be:

– recognition of 12 key words, 50 per cent of the time after Week 1, 75 per cent of the time after Week 2, to recognition of 20 key words 100 per cent of the time within 12 weeks. This will represent complete achievement of the teaching target and the success criteria will reflect this, or not, as the case may be, e.g. if recognition of the key words was only achieved 50 per cent of the time.

It should be clear, therefore, that the success criteria refer to performance which is considered acceptable at different phases of the teaching programme. They represent the milestones and help to break tasks into simpler and smaller steps, providing a measure of the success being achieved. They are a helpful tool for planning and, though they represent the teacher's estimate of what to expect and their assumption of the child's rate of learning, they can be easily modified in the light of teaching and experience.

Outcomes: Include here the actual outcomes or results of the learning programmes. How do these compare with the teaching targets set and the success criteria selected? Were these outcomes as expected? Did they exceed expectations, or were they disappointing?

The support arrangements: Specify in this section who does what, when, how long for and how often? Also include the supervision and monitoring arrangements if teaching is being delegated to another member of staff, especially if this is a learning support assistant (LSA) or teaching assistant (TA). It would be wrong to expect an assistant to deal with a complex learning difficulty on their own and teachers need to remember that this does not absolve them from their responsibility. Times for planning, meetings, or other purposes such as coordinating programmes where a number of people are involved, also require inclusion.

The arrangements for review

It goes without saying that any teaching should be the subject of continuous monitoring and review. However, include here the times and dates for formal planning and reviews between all parties. It might be helpful to differentiate between in-school planning, restricting this to school staff only, and the wider meeting open to parents. The former can take place more frequently and informally, with the focus on planning, intervention and coordination. The latter can then serve to inform and involve parents on what has been achieved and what is outstanding.

Problem analysis

A selection of strategies and approaches

SWOT analysis

In preparing IEPs, a useful approach to adopt is that commonly known as SWOT analysis (see Figure 5.1), from which a plan can be derived. SWOT is shorthand for *Strengths, Weaknesses, Opportunities* and *Threats*. The first two represent the internal processes or characteristics of the problem – those pertaining to the child, e.g. what he can and cannot do. The latter are more to do with external or outside forces, e.g. what the problem represents to a third party, the teaching opportunities and threats faced by the teacher who is trying to help children experiencing difficulties in learning.

SWOT analysis is a useful discipline at the stage of describing the nature of the child's learning difficulty. The *strengths* when identified provide the starting points, the baseline which can be used later to evaluate progress. The *weaknesses* help with the setting of teaching targets. The *opportunities* help focus the teacher's mind on the range of possibilities to try and the *threats* (and obstacles) likely to be encountered and to be dealt with.

The following case study is an example of a SWOT analysis.

Case Study

Rob is a pleasant, sociable and cooperative 15-year-old who was born with congenital abnormalities in his limbs. His upper limbs are only five inches long and he has no hands or fingers, the arms stopping at the elbow. His lower limbs are also short and both end at the knee. He is fitted with prosthetic aids which enable him to be fully mobile so that he can participate fully in most physical activities. He uses his chin and his mouth to handle PE and sports equipment such as a tennis racket. He uses a pencil in his mouth to operate computer equipment and is learning the use of a dictaphone to dictate his work.

Rob attends a mainstream secondary school where he has the support of a part-time learning support assistant. He is making very good progress with his learning and is expected to do well in Computer Studies, English, Maths, Science, Geography, Religious Studies, Drama and French in his GCSE examinations. His main problems are, as expected, in practical activities which require fine motor coordination and these are where he requires the help of the assistant.

Rob has the support of devoted and supportive parents. They are pleased that he is doing so well but are concerned about the future, believing that he will always require additional support as he will be unable to be completely independent.

Rob accepts that there are limitations to the range of opportunities likely to be available to him in the future. However, he is determined to use his strengths in computing to work towards a career in information technology though he is worried that he may not be able to engage in the engineering and repair aspects of working with computers.

SWOT analysis: interpretation and discussion

The SWOT analysis (see Figure 5.1) clearly shows the areas where useful work can be carried out, taking account of the child's strengths and weaknesses. It also helps identify the opportunities for the teacher to use the resources of the child, the parents and other agencies, including LEA support staff. The constraints are also clear: a tight financial budget, the range of realistic possibilities and options for Rob and his need for support due to his inability to be completely independent.

A SWOT analysis helps to focus on the main issues to be addressed in planning and intervention. It enables the teacher to be aware of both the internal and external constraints in planning relating to teachers and children themselves, including other key stakeholders, for example, parents, head teacher, governors and LEA staff. Environmental constraints, such as class size, peer group, community attitudes and school ethos, can be identified. Financial and human resource implications, such as the budgetary situation, availability of support staff, the level of expertise needed, may also be considered.

All of the above are relevant to Rob's education and can be applied in turn to determine the action needed to ensure his continuing, successful integration in the mainstream. Rob represents an excellent and real example of how a child with apparently the most severe and disabling condition can succeed in the mainstream.

PEST analysis

It is usual to combine a SWOT analysis with a PEST analysis. This enables analysis of the wider external environment from a number of perspectives to supplement the SWOT findings which essentially relate to the individual child.

PEST is shorthand for analysis of the *Political, Economic, Sociological* and *Technological* environment. This is normally done at the macro-level, which means looking at issues within the national context – government, politics and attitude, education budgets, values and developments in education, information technology and the use of computers in schools including other technological advances.

PEST analysis ensures an awareness of global issues. It helps focus on the wider context of how external forces dictate practice in the classroom. Teachers may, therefore, wish to think about these issues when preparing their strategies. A modified approach, particularly useful for their purpose, would be to conduct a PEST analysis as it relates to their own circumstances, e.g. their school or LEA, the political structure, practices and attitudes of councillors, governors; budgetary health of their LEA and schools; the community they serve, the support and involvement of parents; the technological resources and expertise available within their school and LEA generally.

Force field analysis

Once the SWOT analysis is completed, teachers might be interested to carry out a further analysis to identify the forces for and against change in respect of either the learner or the environment they are working in. This is known in the

SWOT Analysis	
Strengths	*Weaknesses*
Personality	*Physical disability*
Sociable, cooperative, responsive.	Absence of limbs is a severe handicap, not sufficiently compensated by prosthetic aids. Fine motor tasks cause Rob significant problems.
Determination	*Dependence*
Clear willingness to participate in activities, including those where a physical disability would be a severe handicap.	Rob needs help with some practical activities, especially where safety is a prime consideration.
Ability	*Stamina*
At least average intelligence and able to deal effectively with requirements of mainstream curriculum. Predicted to achieve good grades in GCSE exams.	Rob tires easily and has to put in considerably more effort in his physical activities.
Opportunities	*Threats*
Willing child, supportive parents. Supportive management and Governors.	No clear prognosis about the future. Extent of risk-taking possible: What if anything were to go wrong? Tight financial budget.
Level of cooperation	*Lack of expertise*
Rob has the will to succeed and is prepared to cooperate with teaching arrangements. Active cooperation of LEA staff.	Rob is the only severely disabled child the school has had to provide for. Teachers heavily dependent on other experts.
Use of strengths	*Disability*
Rob has many strengths which could be usefully used to compensate for his physical disability. His communication and cognitive skills can be exploited to the full.	Absence of Rob's limbs makes planning the curriculum difficult. This partially succeeds because of his determination.
The future	*The future*
Rob has a clear vision about the future. This facilitates direction setting, choice of options and decision making, taken in consultation with him.	Rob's aspirations present a challenge. Should be restricted to only those areas in which he is currently succeeding.

Figure 5.1 SWOT Analysis of a child with a physical disability

literature as 'Force field analysis' (see Carnall 1989 for details). It basically represents an attempt to identify the factors pushing for and against change in children's internal and external environments. The Force field diagram (Figure 5.2) shows the forces for and against change for a child experiencing behavioural difficulties in a secondary school.

Forces for change	*Forces for change*
Teacher Need for control in class In the interests of the other children In teacher's own interest	*Child* Wish to improve behaviour Wish to be accepted and seen to be the same as the other children Wish to make progress and waste less time on unproductive behaviours
Expectations of significant others Change required by – head teacher – governing body – parent	*Expectations of significant others* Will not be tolerated for much longer Threat of exclusion Disapproval
Forces against change	*Forces against change*
Teacher Too difficult/time consuming to deal with problem Easier to ask for child to be removed from class Exclusion may be a preferable option long term No resources for this child; demands beyond the teacher/school Child does not fit in with school culture/priorities	*Child* Behaviour leads to attention and status Behaviour is legitimate to deal with perceived injustice Exclusion is one way out of the unbearable situation of school No real expectation of being able to change. School culture alien to child's perceived needs/priorities

Figure 5.2 Force field diagram to show forces for and against change in respect of a child experiencing emotional and behavioural difficulties

Conclusion

It is often the case, as examples in this chapter show, that a child experiences a combination of difficulties in learning, including physical, language, emotional and behavioural problems. In these instances, it is advisable to try to deal with each problem one at a time and, if need be, draw up more than one IEP. This is required as the targets, support arrangements, material and resources are likely to be different, making it cumbersome to include all the information in one document. By using separate documentation for each area, it is easier to plan the workload, ascertain the potential for success with the tasks set and monitor action and progress. The main problem would be with coordination, to avoid duplication or non-attention to the peripheral, overlap areas. However, it should be remembered that the intention of the IEP is to concentrate on the priority problem and to ensure that the focus leads to identifiable results, hence the need to be selective and specific if this focused, concentrated approach is to be maintained.

The following are specimen Individual Education Plans (Specimens A, B and C). Examples of other formats of IEPs are included in Appendices 2 and 3.

Individual Education Plan (Specimen A)

Name: David S   **Date of Birth:** 12.11.92   **School:** XYZ   **Teacher:** Karen D

Strengths and Weaknesses   Priority: Spelling and Writing

Strengths	Weaknesses
David can:	David cannot:
• Read at the level of an eight and half year old	• Write legibly
• Read the books and worksheets used in class	• Spell 90 per cent of words he tries to include in his writing (he has a spelling age of 6 years as assessed on the Vernon Graded Spelling Test)
• Concentrate for a minimum of 5 minutes and up to 10 minutes	• Undertake written work without support/encouragement and does not complete written assignments
• Cooperate and work effectively with his peers	

Teaching Objectives (derived from 1 above)

Objectives	Strategy
David will:	David is to:
• Increase his spelling vocabulary by 5 words a week	• Learn one word a day from list given by class teacher. This will be checked three times a day, twice at school and once at home
• Copywrite one piece of work for 5 minutes daily and must produce at least two lines of legible writing in his book	*Action:* Class teacher to devise teaching approach and to agree strategy with Mrs S
• Complete one written assignment, estimated to require 10 minutes in Week 1, increasing to 12 minutes in Week 2, 14 minutes in Week 3 and 28 minutes by Week 10	• Be shown exactly the standard required and given regular feedback
	Action: Class teacher
	• Be supervised and supported in his efforts by the Special Needs Assistant and will have his work checked by the teacher, on completion

Success Criteria	Contingency Arrangements
• Gains in spelling vocabulary by 5 words a week, David being successful at spelling new words learned 50 per cent of the time on first check, 100 per cent of the time on second check and 100 per cent of the time on third check	• Review targets set, in the light of David's performance
	• Adjust level of supervision/support to match
• Increase in spelling age by 6 to 9 months in school year	• Review/Revise teaching method/strategy and consult with Special Educational Needs Coordinator and/or other colleague if necessary

Provision	Monitoring Arrangements
Materials and resources	• Daily checks and written records for information of all parties
• School's teaching package on spelling	• Weekly planning and review meetings between class teacher and Special Needs Assistant, to include Special Educational Needs Coordinator when necessary
• Books used in class	
• Language master cards for David to use so that he can check spelling on his own	• Weekly communication with Mrs S through note in home/school book
Staffing	• Meeting with Mrs S twice a term
• Special Needs Assistant time	
• Class teacher time (these can be quantified)	

Outcome	
(Record outcome here)	(Date completed):

Individual Education Plan (Specimen B)

Name: John S   Date of Birth: 23.6.92   Date completed: 10.9.00

Nature of Learning Difficulty: Weaknesses in literacy + emotional difficulties
Priority for action: To implement programme for literacy

John has been experiencing problems with his reading and spelling since he joined FL school in September 2000. He has:
- difficulty decoding words and has a sight vocabulary of approximately 10 words (as assessed on list of 100 key words)
- a reading age of 6 years at chronological age 8 years 6 months, placing him at the second centile
- a spelling age of under 6 years, failing to score on the Vernon Graded Word Spelling Test (below the second centile).

He reads very slowly and tends to memorise texts, often making wild guesses. His handwriting is untidy and ill formed. He is able to produce very little work without support: usually two lines of illegible material in 40 minute sessions.

Date of meeting	Present	Action notes
9.9.00	AB, CD, EF, Mrs S	1. Implement literacy programme prepared by Special Educational Needs Coordinator, teacher adviser and class teacher, as agreed with Mrs S

Targets	Success Criteria	Outcome
1. Increase sight vocabulary 2. Enable John to read, through the use of decoding and phonic skills 3. Improve handwriting skills through cursive script	1. Sight vocabulary of 15 words, by December 2000 2. Read one page from his story book, by November 2000 3. Writing is joined up, with spacing and 40 per cent of John's work is legible	

Provision
1. Multi-sensory programme as advised by Specialist Teacher Adviser (STA), using school's reading schemes
1.1. Implementation

Reading
- John is helped with his reading for 15 minutes, twice daily, on a one-to-one basis with Special Needs Assistant (SNA)
- John spends 15 minutes with class teacher in a group of five working on a literacy task
- shared reading at home with his mother for 20 minutes each day

Spelling
- ten minutes each day on Hampshire Special Needs Spelling, with SNA on a one-to-one basis and in small groups
- ten minutes, on his own, working with Talking Pendown
- two words a day to be learned at school, checked at home and rechecked the next day at school; build up to 10 a week (mainly high frequency words)

Handwriting
- ten minutes each day on handwriting practice, copying out list of spelling words learned, with addition of new ones

Monitoring arrangements
Home support
Weekly meetings between:
  SNA/class teacher to plan work,
  check on progress and update
  records

Daily briefing of SNA by teacher,
plus informal contact
Monthly review with Special Educational
Needs Coordinator/STA

Weekly communication with his
mother via home-school book and
termly meetings of approximately
30 minutes at school

Individual Education Plan (Specimen C)

(If behaviour was chosen as a priority, then the following IEP could have been prepared)

Nature of difficulty and priority for action: Behaviour

2. John's behaviour has been deteriorating since around March 2000. This coincides with the break up of the family, his father leaving home and not making contact with him since. He says that he is deeply upset at this and that he is not able to concentrate on his work for longer than a couple of minutes because:

- his mind is on other matters as he worries about his mother's and family's welfare a great deal

- he is failing with his work, being unable to deal with the literacy requirements

- he is distracted by the other children

- he finds that he gets attention when he is 'playing the fool', wandering round the class, shouting out, tearing his work, answering back; this happens on average once hourly

Targets	Success Criteria
1. Improve concentration and cooperative behaviour	1.1. Improved concentration to 5 minutes, for on task behaviour, and 7 minutes, for cooperative behaviour without distracting
	1.2. John works cooperatively with one other person for 5 minutes, by October 2000
	1.3. Tasks estimated to take 15 minutes completed by John within 20 minutes by December 2000
2. Increase periods of time without distracting	2.1. John stays seated for 10 minutes, by October 2000
	2.2. Calling out reduces to twice a day
3. Enable John to:	3.1. John spends 15 minutes daily with teacher and agrees plan for the day – achieves 50 per cent success
- talk about his worries, anxieties and anger	3.2. Use of soft chair as a strategy, reduces frequency of frustration displays by 50 per cent
- follow strategy of removing himself to the soft chair in the classroom to control his frustrations/anger and alert class teacher to his needs	3.3. John takes pride in his achievements and completes 50 per cent of the tasks he is allocated
- improve his self-esteem by being more positive about himself	

6 School Action and School Action Plus

Introduction

The original Code suggested a staged approach in identifying, assessing and providing for children's special educational needs. Five stages were suggested, with Stage 1 being the earliest and Stage 5 representing the point at which special educational needs become the subject of statutory assessment. A number of elements were deemed necessary at each stage. However, the staged approach advocated in the original Code has now been abandoned because of the implication that various stages have to be reached or that hurdles have to be crossed before more intensive help can become available. The revised Code addresses this issue by putting the emphasis where it was always intended to be: that is, at the school level.

There are now simply two levels, both placing action firmly within schools. These are:

1. School Action
2. School Action Plus

These are described below, with an indication of the processes involved, the responsibilities implied and the requirements to be met.

School Action

Initial concern and action: Introduction

School Action should not be viewed as simply having replaced Stages 1 to 3 of the original Code. If this were the case, the revised Code would have stated this. The revision was intended to be much more, partly for the reason stated above, and partly to remind schools of their key roles in making a difference to children's learning. The responsibility for addressing difficulties in learning rests firmly with schools. The roles and support of external agencies are supplementary and complementary; they cannot take over the responsibility; schools retain the accountability and must either take 'action or action plus' as appropriate. Action

Plus serves to show that other agencies either are or have been required to be involved. Schools are required to demonstrate a graduated, carefully constructed approach in their responses at both School Action and School Action Plus.

School Action is required when a learning difficulty is suspected or a concern registered, either from class teachers or from parents. This might have arisen from observation of a child's behaviour or learning, in the sense that normal expectations are not being met. For example, the child may be showing signs of difficulty in comprehending instructions in class, needing to refer back to the teacher for clarification, simplification or even at times for reassurance. Careful assessment and observation might reveal that he is able to respond appropriately to teacher tasks when instructions are given in small groups, on an individual basis or in calm, quiet environments. This might lead to suspicion of a hearing or listening difficulty, especially in young children, and this is when parents need to be contacted or medical notes studied to check on any history of a hearing difficulty. Speed would be of the essence here, if the child is to learn and progress normally.

The point to note is that it is usually individuals with the most direct contact with the child who should notice if something is wrong. This includes other children, support staff, learning support or dining room assistants. In this way, a complete picture of a child's needs within and beyond the school day can be constructed and the basis of the difficulty identified. Questions which could be asked at this stage are:

1. What skills or behaviour should the child be showing at this stage of his development?
2. How far behind is this child compared with his peers? Is this a significant delay and why? Is this affecting relationships with peers?
3. Is the child's attitude and disposition for learning being affected? Does he seem to have problems with access to the curriculum? What can be done to help?
4. How do the parents feel about their child's development or progress? Can they shed any light on the problem?
5. Who is the best person to contact for help?

This list is not meant to be exhaustive but is intended to provide a structured approach towards reflecting upon and making sense of the child's problems. Most of the information should be available without too much effort and normally, at the earlier stages, it will be assumed that the class or subject teacher would have done the groundwork and be in a position to formalise the response the child requires.

Early responses: Summary

Early responses to School Action, following the identification of a learning difficulty, should include the gathering of information; the recording of the child's special educational needs, including the planning and teaching response, and the required consultation with parents. The trigger is when a teacher, parent or other professional gives evidence of concern. Further action is required if, after careful reviews, special help has not resulted in satisfactory progress. If, as in the majority of cases, the child makes sufficient progress, this may serve as confirmation of the progress of the school's action in meeting the child's needs.

The responsibility for assessing children, differentiating teaching and devising appropriate plans remains with the class or subject teacher. They must inform the head teacher, parents and the SENCO and can also ask for help from the SENCO, school doctor, or other professional agency. Referrals may be made to support services, e.g. educational psychologist, school doctors, specialist teachers.

The parents' and child's own views on the learning difficulties must be sought. Any known health, pastoral or social problems should be detailed, together with profiles of achievement, National Curriculum attainments and other information from testing and other forms of assessment, e.g. on school attendance.

Records should be kept of the nature of the concern, the action taken, the targets set and the time when progress is to be reviewed (normally within a term or six months, with parents kept informed).

Recognition of need for 'intensive' action

If progress is not forthcoming, this would imply the existence of a persistent learning difficulty, requiring intensive teaching and support. This will require more detailed assessment and advice, leading to the provision of regular and systematic help. The cycle of assessing, teaching and reviewing should be more systematically monitored, with more frequent evaluation of teaching and review with regard to the efficacy of the teaching approaches and arrangements, including the appropriateness of the learning material. IEPs should be prepared at this stage, following consultation and with the active involvement of parents and, as much as possible, the pupils themselves.

Questions to ask are:

Learning difficulties
What is now known about the learning difficulty?
  What methods have been tried and which ones have been more successful?
  Are there any areas where practice could be improved?

Priority
What is the priority area for attention and remediation?
  Does this need to be broken down into sub-areas so that manageable objectives can be set?

Teaching strategy
Why did the child not respond to the earlier arrangements?
  Where are adjustments/revisions required?
  Should the focus be more on the child's learning style or greater differentiation of the curriculum?
  Should teaching be in even smaller steps?

Staffing arrangements

What staffing arrangements need to be made to provide the child with the intensive help that he needs?

How will this help be secured, organised, monitored and evaluated?

Most children should respond to the more sytematic arrangements necessary at the later stages of School Action, bearing in mind that they would have attracted an increasingly focused, differentiated teaching approach to deal with their learning difficulty as soon as this had been identified. Evaluation of their progress would normally be made at their IEP reviews and decisions on whether or not they need more intensive help, perhaps at School Action Plus, can be made following two consecutive reviews.

Intensive help within School Action: Summary

The increasingly graduated approach expected within School Action encompasses the seeking and provision of further assessment and advice, including the creation of an Individual Education Plan, with a view to implementing *intensive* help.

Process

The SENCO takes the lead in assessing the child's learning difficulty, planning a programme of intervention and monitoring and supporting its delivery. This will assist in reviewing and evaluating the effectiveness of the teaching arrangements and the provision made. The SENCO may seek additional information or advice from Health, Social Services or other agencies after consultation with parents, and agree appropriate action with them and with the child's teachers. A review should take place within two terms to which parents should be invited; they must be consulted and appropriately advised if school staff are planning to move towards School Action Plus.

Requirements

An IEP must be drawn up and this should set out the nature of the child's learning difficulty, specific learning targets and the materials and resources to be used, including any special provision. The staff to be involved and the frequency of support to be made, including the timescale within which work is to be carried out, should be specified. The monitoring and assessment arrangements and the date for review should also be agreed.

School Action Plus

Early intensive help with external support

School Action Plus applies to a small minority of children whose needs are so complex as to require even more help than the intensive arrangements available during School Action. In terms of the 'Warnock 20 per cent' (DES 1978), these children are likely to be functioning towards the bottom end of the range, towards the 2 per cent of children who experience special educational needs.

This does not mean that they will be in the bottom 2 per cent in all areas. Their educational profile should show strengths in some areas and weaknesses in the development of the skills calling for remediation, e.g. a 14-year-old who has achieved Level 7 of the National Curriculum in Maths and Science but who is struggling with spelling and presentation of his work though able to deal with the reading components of the curriculum. Obviously, these difficulties would have been identified earlier and provided for through the support available during School Action. It is only when they prove to be persistent and resistant to teaching and remediation that School Action Plus processes would be called for. The clear implication is that previous action would have demonstrated careful and systematic planning, collaboration between teachers and others and creativity on the teacher's part in trying a number of measures targeted at the area of concern. It is not necessary to wait for School Action Plus in order to use external specialist help and advice; this can and should be done at any time if considered useful. It is better to tackle a problem early than to wait.

At School Action Plus, external agencies are routinely called in and they would wish to establish that support has been made available over a period of time and has been systematically and appropriately implemented. This is to ascertain that the teaching programmes and other forms of intervention have indeed been exhausted. Sometimes they are not, and some adjustments may be needed. They would also wish to check that intervention has been based on comprehensive assessment, with documentation available to assist with further planning and evaluation. This is particularly important with regard to children who experience emotional and behavioural difficulties. Such documentation should have a balanced focus. For example, it would be inappropriate to have detailed records of incidents relating to the child's unacceptable behaviour, without equivalent information on the steps and strategies taken to deal with the problem.

The necessary information relating to a child's difficulty should be available, e.g. medical information about a physical or sensory problem, even though these may be mild and easily overlooked. Mild clumsiness, loss of concentration and periods of inattention, lack of spontaneous response, twitching of muscles and restlessness in class may all be significant but may not have been explored fully, with the school doctor for example. Similarly, home circumstances may not be well-known to the teacher, e.g. parents' illnesses, domestic circumstances. Marriage break-up may have a considerable effect on the child's learning and needs to be taken into account when planning teaching programmes.

Teachers might wish to ask the following questions, if considering whether a child's needs require measures at School Action Plus:

Nature of learning difficulty
Are the child's needs so complex as to require significantly more help and a different type of approach to that provided earlier?

Teaching and assessment
Have the teaching interventions been systematically planned and given sufficient time to work?

Have these been based on concrete evidence of assessment? Give details.
Which areas of the child's functioning seem to be more resistant to change?

Priorities for action and performance indicators
What are the priority areas to address?
What would serve as useful indicators to monitor and evaluate progress?

Consensus on learning difficulty
What is the consensus of opinion on the child's learning difficulty?
Do the children, their parents, teachers or support staff feel that: (a) appropriate and (b) sufficient help has been given?

Consultation with teachers
Have all teachers been consulted? (It is essential in secondary schools to consult with teachers and establish their views.) In which areas do they feel the child is doing well? Which strategies are more likely to bear fruit?

Consultation with parents
How do parents feel about the whole process?
Do they believe they have been adequately consulted/involved?

Consultation with the child
How does the child feel?
Does the child understand and is he committed to the plan?
Does the child consider it realistic and what level of responsibility is he prepared and able to accept?

Standards setting and contingency planning
Have expectations and standards been clearly specified? Give details.
Which support structures are required to facilitate achievement of these?
What are the contingency arrangements to deal with problems, failures and unplanned events?

These questions are set out in the style of a usable form in Appendix 5.

Summary

The school calls on outside specialist help.

Process
The responsibility for pupils experiencing special educational needs is shared between the class teacher, the SENCO and outside support teachers such as specialist teacher advisers or educational psychologists. These external agencies may offer classroom support, advice on teaching approaches, materials, technology or classroom management or indeed direct teaching. Reviews are organised by the SENCO within one or two terms to include and involve parents (and where possible the child), focus on progress made, report on effectiveness of the

IEP and update information in the light of progress made. Future plans can be discussed and agreed. If progress is not satisfactory, the head teacher, in consultation with all parties involved, may consider referring the child to the LEA for a statutory assessment.

Requirements

An IEP must have been completed, following consultation and advice from support services. Following on from School Action Plus, a range of documentation and evidence will be required to support a referral to the LEA for statutory assessment, should this be needed. This should:

– include educational and developmental profiles
– summarise the views of the parents and of the child
– itemise any health or social factor likely to have an influence on the child's learning
– show evidence of strategies tried and the progress achieved
– demonstrate a coordinated approach in the planning and teaching response, including the involvement of professionals with relevant knowledge and expertise outside the normal competence of the school
– show evidence of consistent and systematic delivery of the teaching and other approaches agreed, including effective use of any special resources targeted for the child
– emphasise and demonstrate the effectiveness of the teaching input as opposed to searching for within-child factors to explain lack of progress
– show evidence of a planned and coordinated intervention over time.

Considering the need for statutory assessment

Seeking statutory assessment represents the point at which action ceases to be wholly school based. This is when schools and the LEA have to cooperate and share responsibility in assessing and providing for children experiencing special educational needs. This stage is reached if it is considered that the child's needs should be subject to the statutory assessment procedures laid down by the 1996 Education Act. It does not mean, however, that the assessment will necessarily lead to the production of a Statement of Special Educational Needs. This has caused much confusion in the past, not helped by the use of such terms as 'Statementing'. What essentially happens at the statutory assessment stage is the collection of professional advice and evidence by the LEA to enable it to make a decision on whether or not to proceed with statutory assessment.

If the LEA decides to proceed, it will request advice and evidence from a range of professionals, including parents, doctors, teachers, social workers and educational psychologists as to how best to provide for a child experiencing special educational needs. If, on the other hand, it decides that there is no basis to initiate a statutory assessment, it has to give reasons as to why not within a specified time limit. The time limit does not apply if the request originated from somewhere other than from the parents or the school.

Statutory assessment therefore represents a process which ensues when a child is referred to the LEA so that it may determine the SEN and the provision required. It goes without saying that the responsibilities identified at previous stages would be ongoing and would require to be met, irrespective of the LEA's decision on whether or not to proceed with statutory assessment.

Completion of statutory assessment

This stage is reached when the LEA has agreed that there is prima facie evidence for statutory assessment and has collected advice from the professionals mentioned above. The LEA then has one of two options. This may be to conclude that the child's needs can be met from the resources already available at school, or to determine to provide the child with a Statement of Special Educational Needs.

If the LEA chooses the first option it may provide a note in lieu of a Statement of Special Educational Needs. This will detail the child's special educational needs and the provision needed to meet them, including broad educational objectives and other requirements deemed necessary. Other reports and other evidence submitted during the statutory assessment will also be made available to the parents. However, the main difference between the first and second options is that in the former the provision to be made has to come from resources already available to the school. The aim in both cases will, however, be the same: to provide and meet the child's needs, as identified, fully and appropriately.

With the second option, the LEA provides a Statement of Special Educational Needs. This is a legal document which is in six parts. Part 1 lists the biographical details. Part 2 details the special educational needs, including the child's strengths and weaknesses, levels of functioning and a summary of the requirements. Part 3 focuses on the special education provision to be made, including details of broad teaching objectives, the level of staffing support to be made available and the monitoring and review arrangements. Part 4 specifies the school or other arrangement required by the child, including the name of the school. Part 5 details the non-educational needs and Part 6 deals with any non-educational provision required, e.g. physiotherapy, speech therapy.

Statutory assessment and beyond

It cannot be too strongly stressed that during and beyond the statutory assessment procedures, there are clear responsibilities on schools to provide for children experiencing special educational needs, especially when these are reinforced in a Statement of Special Educational Needs. Statements, when provided, represent legal documents, the bases of contracts between the LEA and the school with the parents and their child experiencing special educational needs. The requirements contained within them must be fully understood and provided for by the relevant parties. Arrangements must also be made to report on progress, normally within the structure of the Annual Reviews. These are formal meetings designed to revise and update Statements while at the same time reporting on progress achieved. Chapter 7 deals with the statutory assessment procedures; Chapter 8 considers the Annual Review process in cases where Statements are issued by the LEA, and Chapter 9 details the procedures which operate for children with Statements at Year 9 and beyond.

7 Statutory assessment

Introduction

There will be a number of children who do not make satisfactory progress, in spite of remedial teaching and support over the long term. This is estimated to be around 2 per cent of the school population and represents those experiencing the most severe, long-term or complex needs. Their identification, assessment and the eventual level of help they are provided with will vary according to a number of circumstances, the most significant of which is the school they are in and its approach to providing for special educational needs. The level of teacher expertise and resources available, including voluntary help, the needs of the child and the support parents and others are able to offer are also significant.

Teacher tasks

Teachers would be expected to demonstrate systematic planning and teaching if there is any intention of a child being referred to the LEA for statutory assessment. This is expected at all times and is particularly important at the statutory assessment stage, when a decision is being made that a child's needs are so significant and complex as to call for a multi-disciplinary assessment under the 1996 Education Act. Given that teachers would need to advise the 'responsible person', i.e. the person responsible for special educational needs in the school, they would need to ensure that they are able to provide sound reasoning, with evidence to support their request for statutory assessment. It would not be sufficient to assert that a child is not learning or progressing. Instead, it would need to be demonstrated how and why progress is incapable of being made within all the arrangements that have been made available. Referring back to the graduated approaches within School Action and School Action Plus, it is clear that significant and intensive levels of support would have been made available, including specialist advice outside of the school. Therefore, a sound appreciation of the criteria which apply at the statutory assessment stage and beyond is required if an effective response is to be achieved. It will be noted that decisions regarding requests for statutory assessment rest with the LEA, whose officers will be guided by factors pertaining to children as well as circumstances within and beyond school.

Criteria for statutory assessment

The following questions are likely to be asked when assessing the need for statutory assessment.

The child
1. When was the child identified as experiencing a learning difficulty and what has been his response over time to teaching and other intervention?
2. Are there baselines recorded as to what the child can and cannot do? For example, can the child now walk, talk, read, and write at a level that he could not do at the appropriate developmental stages? Are the child's abilities, as measured, at or below the second centile, e.g. in terms of cognitive abilities – memory, reasoning, problem solving? Or does reading, spelling and number ability fall significantly below that expected for a child of his age? What are the child's National Curriculum attainments? Is there a significant discrepancy between those and what would normally be expected from his peers?
3. What is the child's level of maturity with regard to social, emotional and moral development? Is the child safe in a school environment, can he be trusted outside without constant supervision? Is the child a danger to himself or to others? Is the child socially and emotionally well adjusted? Is he able to integrate with peers and within school generally? Is the child easily misled or made the scapegoat? Is the child confident, articulate, able to express his point of view, or withdrawn, nervous, unusually shy and reticent?
4. What are the child's self-help and physical skills, and independence with regard to feeding, toileting? Can the child change for PE, tie his own shoelaces, participate in physical activities? Or is he slow, clumsy, prone to falls and vulnerable? Does the child require a differentiated sequence of activities that take into account his physical and safety needs? Is the child able to manage steps, stairs, distance? Is he safe with equipment?
5. Does the child have any medical problems? Does he have epilepsy or asthma? What physical activities need care in the light of these, e.g. excessive exertion, swimming, climbing? Is medication and/or physiotherapy required at regular intervals during the day, e.g. for cystic fibrosis, cerebral palsy? What are the child's needs for privacy and can the school provide for these?
6. What are the curriculum requirements? Can these be reasonably differentiated by task and by outcome?

The teacher
1. What arrangements have been made in the past to support the child's teaching, and how effective have these been? What changes are required and can these be made within the school's existing resources?

2. What are the immediate tasks, demands and pressures on the teacher? Do these make it unrealistic to provide the kinds of programmes required by the child?

3. Does the teacher have the level of experience and/or expertise required, including the confidence to provide for the child's needs? For example, many teachers need reassurance and support – including advice, training and guidance – if they are to successfully deal with a learning difficulty outside of their range of expertise. This is often the case with mainstream teachers confronted with the problems of autism or mutism in the classroom, or when dealing with children experiencing speech and language disorders requiring signing and other forms of non-verbal communication. The inclusion of children experiencing severe learning difficulties in the mainstream, e.g. Down's syndrome or tubero sclerosis, creates challenges (see Buckley and Bird 1994, Ware 1994). The benefits they derive from inclusion have also been well documented (Buckley 2000).

The school

1. Does the school have demonstrated expertise in the area or a strong track record of innovation and successful initiatives, including strong leadership with regard to special educational needs?

2. Are resources already targeted to the school for a specific purpose? Is it a resourced school for children with either physical disabilities or visual or hearing impairment? This will only affect the decision for statutory assessment if the child is already at the school and, say, requires a lift or special tables, that is the facilities would ordinarily have been available without a Statement being necessary. It should not enter the equation if it means the school needing to reallocate resources, e.g. close circuit TV provided for children with Statements, or teaching inputs from specialist teachers available from special units on campus.

3. What are the special needs resources already delegated to the school? What are children's entitlements in relation to their individual special needs? Alternatively, how are special needs resources organised – to provide for smaller classes, small teaching groups or extra special needs staffing?

The LEA

1. What arrangements does the LEA already have in order to support a specific type of special need? Does it already provide a specialist team of teacher advisers?

2. What flexibilities exist in terms of funding, advice or placement, to provide for children whose difficulties are not likely to be long term, severe or complex?

3. What are the requirements of local schools with respect to provision for a specific type of need? How can these be jointly provided or facilitated between schools to make effective use of resources, where, for example, the needs of a hearing or visually impaired child requiring special facilities are such that it would not make economic sense to make adjustments for that child alone?

4. Does it make sense to maintain a specific pool of expertise to service specific areas of needs for schools to buy in, e.g. specialist teachers for language or for specific learning difficulties?

Teachers would need to be aware of the above criteria in order to be able to submit evidence and professional advice in support of statutory assessment. LEAs normally provide guidance on the information required and the forms used to either request statutory assessment or provide Educational Advice, including a structure which could be usefully followed.

Some LEAs have moved forward, combining the request for statutory assessment and the provision of Educational Advice into one step. This saves duplicating work but has implications.

The advice submitted must be clear, comprehensive, accurate and up to date, supported with concrete, objective evidence of the child's learning difficulties and the interventions attempted, with details of the outcome. There are also some essential requirements to be met. The school needs to provide a summary of the steps taken to support the child at School Action and School Action Plus. This should include information on the nature of the management approaches adopted, on how the curriculum was differentiated and on the monitoring arrangements used, including the educational outcome achieved.

A balanced picture of the child's functioning in all areas is needed. This means including details of the child's strengths and weaknesses, interests and aptitudes. These need not be confined to school only – a child may excel at athletics but struggle with reading.

Comparative assessments are important. How does the child compare with his peers? What objective information and assessments exist to show how he is performing compared with his peers? It is also helpful to include an indication of the child's and parents' views, including information relating to any special circumstances, e.g. details of health, welfare, attendance, and other information which may be appropriate. Have other professionals been involved? If so, what are their views?

Decisions relating to statutory assessment will be based on whether or not the school requires resources, 'additional to, or otherwise different from' the facilities ordinarily available. These facilities include funds already delegated to schools so that they may meet their obligations at School Action and School Action Plus. Some LEAs (e.g. Southampton, Hampshire and Portsmouth) have delegated resources for this purpose, based on a Special Educational Needs Audit (see L6 under Hampshire publications in the Further reading and references section). Others may have adopted a 'banding system' whereby resources are allocated according to the Stage the child had reached under the original Code of Practice; this will obviously be revised. There is no real difference in either approach as, in essence, resources are matched to the level of need based on a predetermined formula. Teachers, however, need to be aware of the agreed practices in their LEA as requests for statutory assessment will not normally be successful unless it can be demonstrated that resources additional to or different from those available at School Action and School Action Plus are needed.

Preparation and submission of the Educational Advice

It can be seen that the statutory Educational Advice requires a great deal of preparation, care and thought. It should not be entertained until the required evidence and documentation can be marshalled into a logical, coherent argument which shows exactly why statutory assessment is necessary.

The following provides a suggested checklist ranging from the pre-requirements to completion of the Educational Advice submitted as part of the statutory assessment process.

Pre-requirements

The main problems which sometimes arise relate to omission of any evaluation of the school based action and the absence of relevant documentation, a problem which should have normally been resolved through careful use of Individual Education Plans. There is often an inclination to proceed too early and too quickly to the next step of considering statutory assessment. This is understandable when the child is clearly perceived not to be progressing and when inadequacies of resources are considered to be at fault. However, attempts to adjust plans, arrangements and curricula may in future be required, falling in with the action required by the Code of Practice.

Other issues arise from a confusion over the definition of terms. The most common and problematic relates to the school's perceptions and responses to the LEA's invitation to comment on the 'resources and provision' required by the child. This is inevitably perceived as requiring a comment on the level of staffing required. This is unhelpful, especially when strong recommendations are made about alternative provision. These have the effect of raising parental expectations and often pre-empt the whole assessment procedure.

It is not difficult to understand why some schools respond in the way they do – which is perfectly logical when viewed from their perspective. Their circumstances are urgent and pressing and, after all, they have the responsibility of delivering the goods to the child already *in situ*. However, they need to ensure that the problems listed in the foregoing paragraphs do not arise. This will serve to reduce delay and ensure that their requirements are processed more speedily. The Code makes it a clear requirement for the LEA to specify in Part 4 of the Statement the level of additional assistance to be made available to the child in terms of teaching or special needs assistance support. This is a function for the LEA. Some already 'band' children's needs in categories relating to specified levels and quantities for support. Others rely on advice from their professional advisers, including schools.

A common problem relates to the process of quantification, which is extremely complex. The temptation is to opt for the ideal situation in the absence of a detailed breakdown of the requirements relating to the purpose for which additional help is to be used. There have been, of course, guidelines from the DFE (Circular 11/90). These attempt to provide a formula by which resources can be determined: for example, 0.1 Qualified Teacher Assistance (QTA) and 0.1 Special Needs Assistance for a child experiencing moderate learning difficulties, and minor deviations from this range for children experiencing severe learning difficulties or emotional and behavioural difficulties. These are, of course, for guidance only, with adjustments to be made once a definite view has been formed of the needs of the child on completion of the statutory assessment.

This implies that careful consideration is given to the nature and extent of the child's learning difficulties, including his educational circumstances and those which pertain in the school. The decision relating to the quantification of resources should normally be made at the very end of the statutory assessment to enable a complete view of the difficulties, following examination of all the perspectives included in the written advice submitted as part of the statutory assessment, also known as appendices relating to the statutory assessment process. It follows that this should not be pre-empted by decisions being taken too early.

Some problems which have arisen in the past have related to the recommendation of a level of support in appendices, not confirmed on completion of assessment. This is often related to a number of reasons, among which are the requirement on the LEA to make efficient and effective use of its resources and a commitment to pursue a policy of inclusion. It also has to be accountable for public funds; determining the precise requirements for supporting children in schools in a consistent and equitable way enhances this process.

The task for schools
Schools could assist this process by clearly defining their proposals in the Appendix B or Educational Advice. They could detail:

- the type and frequency of the educational programmes they are proposing as their intervention
- the type of material they would need to prepare, e.g. for a child with a visual impairment
- the safety arrangements that are necessary, e.g. around the school, in the playground, during PE and in Science.

They should also confirm the consultation and review arrangements.

This information can then be considered with the rest in the other appendices to determine the likely frequency, intensity, duration and implementation of the interventions necessary. The danger that may result from one party specifying too soon the level of support is inadequate resourcing because other problems were not known except by other contributors. There is also the problem of raising expectations and the possibility of the information being used to apportion blame if the child fails to make the expected progress. This is becoming quite frequent, forming parental responses to Annual Reviews where they feel, strongly and with some justification, that their child's chances of progress have been denied because of inadequate resourcing compared to what was recommended by one professional.

Finally, the other main and very frequent complication that tends to occur relates to the type of provision a child needs. Teachers sometimes feel that a child is inappropriately placed in their school for particular reasons. While this is acceptable, the issue becomes confounded when generalisations are made, based on inadequate evidence. The most common error is to assume that a child who has not coped in one school will have the same problems elsewhere if the type of establishment is similar. Difficulties which have often resulted when making specific placement recommendations have been in terms of shutting doors to the child with regard to securing an alternative placement, constraining the Authority into making one type of placement as opposed to another and denying parental choice (Ramjhun 2001). These open the possibility of litigation on the basis that the child's future has been prejudiced (see, for instance, Harris 1997). The following case study illustrates this.

Case Study

Jane is an 11-year-old who was recently issued with a Statement of Special Educational Needs. The Educational Advice submitted by her school says that she experiences emotional and behavioural difficulties, making it unlikely that she will be able to cope in the mainstream. The other appendices do not support this view and therefore the Statement, while acknowledging that Jane has difficulties, proposes that her needs should continue to be met in the mainstream. A number of objectives have been set and additional support in the form of learning support assistance has been agreed.

However, Jane has been refused a place at her local secondary school to which she was to transfer in the following term and the LEA has been asked to intervene by the parents. The head teacher of the secondary school is concerned that his primary school colleagues have advised against continuation in the mainstream and he has the full support of his governing body. On the other hand, the parents argue that none of the other contributors see the need for a placement other than in the mainstream. This includes the educational psychologist and the multi-disciplinary body which sat on the LEA's behalf to confirm that placement in the mainstream is appropriate. (Cases of this kind abound in LEAs (Ramjhun 2001); they are extremely costly in terms of time and the various meetings and deliberations needed. They also leave parties open and vulnerable to litigation.)

In Jane's case, her parents sought an alternative mainstream placement and asked the LEA to provide the transport. The alternative secondary schools approached refused admission on the grounds that the child's local school should seriously reconsider; one felt that mainstream education was out of the question. In the event, the parents no longer wanted anything more to do with their local schools, both the primary and secondary schools, feeling aggrieved with them.

The LEA was forced into finding a solution acceptable to all parties. Therefore, what started as a genuine concern about how to provide for Jane backfired to the extent that she was still without a school place at the start of her secondary education.

This case serves to highlight how genuine concerns can backfire and cause a 'ripple effect' with unexpected consequences. A lesson that should be learned is the vulnerability of parents and the child in respect of recommendations and decisions made by third parties, sometimes with dire consequences concerning their future. Extreme care should be taken to avoid pre-empting the outcome of the statutory assessment; this will avoid confusion, conflict and uncertainty, which only serve to cause delays and work against the child's best interests.

Conclusions

Statutory assessments represent complex procedures. Parents with little or no knowledge of these procedures may find the process daunting and will be anxious to ensure that they are able to safeguard their child's best interests. Knowing how best to contribute and to collaborate on equal terms would be a challenge many of them would wish to be setting themselves and it would be helpful for them to have every assistance to succeed. This is where the LEA's adviser will have a useful role, particularly in regard to explaining the processes to be followed, including details of parental rights at each stage. Help could also be available from the Parent Partnership Officer or adviser to the parents. Together, they could be assisted to make sense of and respond effectively to the volume of documentation which follows completion of the statutory assessment procedures.

In particular, parents should be advised of their rights to contribute to the assessment by providing their own Parental Advice and/or Parental Representation, which is advice prepared by a friend, relative or more frequently, professional adviser (see Glossary). They may have meetings with an officer of the LEA if they are unhappy with the contents and proposals in the proposed Statement, i.e. the Statement before it is signed and finalised as a legal document. They can also secure independent advice from their advisers. They may additionally involve their local Parent Partnership Service or Mediation Service; LEAs are required to inform them of the facilities available to them in their area.

Parents should be told of the importance of observing the time limits that apply at each stage of the assessment process, e.g. 29 days within which to submit their advice and evidence from the date of the start of statutory assessment, and 15 days between meetings at proposed Statement stage. If, in spite of consultations between parents and LEA officers, an agreement cannot be reached on any aspect of the Statement, the former have a right of appeal to an SEN Tribunal. The time limit for such appeals is two months following the date when the Statement is signed and finalised by an authorised LEA officer.

8 Annual Reviews

Purposes of Annual Reviews

Annual Reviews are required at least once a year in order to review and update the Statement of Special Educational Needs. More frequent reviews may be required if the child's needs or circumstances change rapidly. Annual Reviews are essentially about reviewing the past, looking at the present and planning the future. Their main purposes are to review progress made over the preceding year, identify outstanding tasks and agree future objectives, both new ones and those set previously and not completely achieved. They serve to review needs and to update the Statement in the light of this; levels of provision can also be adjusted and the appropriateness of placement considered. Recommendations must also be made on whether or not to continue to maintain the Statement. While Annual Reviews are organised and conducted at school, these can only make recommendations; it is for the LEA to make decisions. This is not always understood by parents and other parties so that Chairs of Annual Reviews are advised to make this clear (DfES 2001b).

How to get the best out of Annual Reviews

Annual Reviews provide an ideal opportunity to consult with parents and to formalise plans in order to continue to provide the appropriate support and help to childrren. However, they can also be rather formal and daunting occasions to parents as well as teachers. When this happens, a valuable opportunity is lost for close cooperation between both parties. An atmosphere of trust can be generated with effective and sensitive chairing of these meetings, a task often falling to the head teacher, at times assisted by the LEA representative, usually the Educational Psychologist. A great deal of work could and should also have been done beforehand to reassure parents and make them feel welcome and valued as equal partners in the process. If children are also invited, then the process of the meeting takes on even greater importance, greatly helped by advance planning. It should be remembered, of course, that children have a right to attend their Annual Reviews and they should be given every encouragement and support to do so. However, the task of empowering them to make an effective contribution is daunting and a real challenge to schools. This will be covered later in this chapter.

The following is normally found helpful at Annual Reviews.

Physical arrangements

Seating should be organised beforehand to allow parents and child to sit next to each other, preferably opposite the chairperson but near to the class teacher or other person familiar to them. Individuals representing authority, e.g. LEA representative, head teacher, should not bunch together. Sitting behind desks should be avoided. The meeting should be held in a spacious room, preferably with comfortable chairs. There should be a notice not to be disturbed once the meeting has started.

Process

The chairperson should introduce himself or herself and invite others to do so. He or she should briefly outline the agenda, including the purpose of the Review, reminding all parties of the contents in Parts 2 and 3 of the Statement Cover, i.e. special educational needs and special educational provision.

The class teacher, SENCO or head teacher then reports on objectives set previously and the progress achieved. Parents are invited to respond and express their views and thoughts on any matter which they want to share or discuss. Most parents are articulate and able to contribute or even lead the meeting but there are some who need reassurance and encouragement. These parents should not be asked direct questions until they have had an opportunity to listen and to 'warm' to the discussion. There are many instances when they may feel intimidated or marginalised, needing to be brought in and actively encouraged to contribute to the meeting. This should already be known to the chairperson and in these instances, the Parent Partnership service should have been involved.

Jargon should be avoided. If any educational terminology is used, it is important to ensure that parents understand what it means. If not, an explanation is required. This applies in particular to National Curriculum terminology which may be meaningless to parents. For example, what does it mean if an 11-year-old child is functioning at Level 1 of the National Curriculum? Parents will, however, place this in context if they are told that most 11-year-olds are achieving at Levels 4 and 5 of the National Curriculum; this will enable them to make a comparison of their child's attainments with the appropriate peer group.

Requirements for Review meetings

A copy of the Statement and of the latest Annual Review, if one has been carried out, should be available at the meeting. The minimum information that will be required from these relates to the child's special educational needs and the special educational provision being made; this will help to establish whether the child's special educational needs remain the same, whether some have changed and whether new ones have arisen. This will detail the objectives set and being worked towards; this is necessary in order to determine the extent to which progress has been made and the extent to which they have been achieved. Any written information provided by parties unable to attend the Review should also be considered and this should normally have been made available to the parents well in advance of the meeting.

An agenda for schools

A useful agenda which schools might use is included in the Code of Practice and in the SEN Toolkit (DfES 2001a, 2001b). The following questions should be addressed:

- What are the parents' views of the past year's progress and their aspirations for the future?
- What are the pupil's views of the past year's progress and his aspirations for the future?
- What is the school's view of the child's progress over the past year? What has been the child's progress towards meeting the overall objectives in the Statement? What success has the child achieved in meeting the targets set?
- Have there been significant changes in the child's circumstances which affect his development and progress?
- Is current provision, including the National Curriculum, or arrangements substituted for it, appropriate to the child's needs?
- What educational targets should be adopted against which the child's educational progress will be assessed during the coming year and at the next Review?
- Is the Transition Plan helping the pupil's progress to adult life?
- Is any further action required and, if so, by whom?
- Does the Statement remain appropriate?
- Are any amendments to the Statement required or should the LEA be recommended to cease to maintain it?

There is one problem worth noting here and this is with the ordering of the questions. In some cases, especially when parents need to 'warm up' to the meeting, it would be more appropriate to start with teachers and others detailing their views and informing parents and the child that they will have an opportunity to respond and comment afterwards. If need be, they may even ask immediately for clarification of any point or issue.

Agenda for parents

In asking parents to give their 'views of the past year's progress and their aspirations for the future', the following simplification may be found helpful by all parties:

- what progress has been noted by parents in the past year in respect of
  - behaviour and relationships
  - interest and motivation
  - attitude to learning
  - cooperation with parents at home
  - perseverance with tasks
  - attainments and skills development;
- what has pleased them;
- what continues to cause them concern and any suggestions to deal with this;
- any significant events which might have affected their child's progress;
- what they would like to see achieved during the next year.

Parents can be forewarned about the type of questions they will be asked, with advice and guidance in respect of the contributions expected of them. Some authorities, e.g. Southampton and Hampshire, produce an Annual Review leaflet which explains the Annual Review in sufficient detail to enable effective parental contribution.

Essential issues to be addressed at Annual Reviews

The Annual Review should, at minimum, cover the following.

The past

- Exactly what progress has been achieved during the past year?
- How does the intervention provided match with the needs identified in the Statement?
- How appropriate were the teaching objectives which were set and have they been achieved? If so, to what extent?
- Have outcomes been measured and recorded?

The present

- What are the most important needs of the child now and in what priority order?
- What needs to be done, by whom, by when and how?
- Is there anything new that has come to light and how is it best to plan and provide for this?
- What constitute short and medium term targets and can these be agreed?

The future

- What are the long term plans for the child?
  - independent study skills, cooperative behaviour, fluent and accurate reading and spelling
  - attainment targets comparable to the child's peers, GCSE success

 – development of life skills, independence, social skills
 – vocational placement, work employment.

Recommendations to the LEA and parents

This relates essentially to the following:
- Are the child's needs being appropriately met?
- Does the school placement remain appropriate?
- Is there any change needed in the nature or level of the special educational provision?
- Does the Statement need to be maintained?

Including children at their Annual Review meetings

Children have a right to attend their Annual Reviews and should therefore be included as far as possible. It is, however, acknowledged that there are some difficulties and concerns to be addressed if their inclusion is to be effective and not counter-productive. These arise when information to be discussed at Annual Reviews is of a highly sensitive nature, best not fully disclosed to the child, e.g. a terminal illness, predicted consequences of other medical diagnoses in terms of learning and/or physical deterioration or any uncertainties which are likely to cause unnecessary worry and anxiety. The same applies to reports containing information which may have a harmful effect on the child's self-image and self-esteem or which could cause unnecessary embarrassment, e.g. ability levels, unsociable behaviour. On these occasions, parents or other parties may wish to have time to share information in confidence in order to minimise the risk of causing anxiety, embarrassment or distress to the child.

However, when the above applies, it should be possible to include the child in the deliberations of the Annual Review, with some adjustments and fine tuning in relation to the timing, duration of attendance, preparation and support at the meeting. The more able and confident the child, the more effective they are likely to be at their Reviews.

In preparing children for Annual Reviews, the following is helpful:

1. Explain to children well beforehand that there is to be a meeting about how they are being helped in school, i.e. remove the focus from children's weaknesses and emphasise the strategies in operation.

2. Explain that their parents are being invited to attend.

3. Provide guidance to parents as to how their children are being prepared for the Annual Review so that they can help too, by being consistent in their approach and in the way they share information.

4. Tell the children how many adults will be at the review and who they are. Explain what is expected and reassure them by explaining how they are to be supported. Explain that they may contribute as much or as little as they wish and that they may choose just to listen to the discussion and proposals.

5. Explain the procedure as clearly as possible – what happens; why it is necessary to look at reports and statements; how long the meeting lasts and which

part they will be attending. Avoid jargon and explain in language understandable to them such terms as Statement, Annual Review, objectives and provision.
6. Explain that their point of view matters and that they are not expected to necessarily agree with what is being said. They can ask for clarification on any point or indeed challenge any inaccuracy. They can also suggest ways in which they would like to work or be helped.
7. Prepare children for the kinds of questions to be asked at the Review. Explain what these mean and the kinds of information being looked for.
8. Ascertain the children's views and relay these on their behalf, if they are unable or unwilling to do so at the meeting. Ensure that they are willing for this to happen prior to the meeting.
9. Do not keep children waiting. Include them at the beginning and, unless they wish to attend the whole meeting, tell them how long they will be attending for.
10. Explain that they will have full information from their parents and teachers in respect of decisions made at the meeting if they are not able to be present for the whole proceedings. Also, that where parents are unable to be present, an adviser, friend or advocate can represent them.

Annual Review documentation

As should be clear by now, there are some key requirements needed for effective Annual Reviews. The documentation that arises from these is as important, representing the only records of the meeting. This information, if properly collected and recorded, provides an extremely useful planning document which should be kept 'live and active', influencing teaching and any other action throughout the year during which it remains in force. However, its completion can be daunting to the inexperienced and a specimen Annual Review report is given at the end of this chapter.

Annual Reviews and school reports

The question is often asked by teachers as to whether it is best to combine the Annual Review with the school report to parents. This is in an attempt to reduce the time required in administration and production of these reports in addition to the necessary meetings with parents. In considering the best response, it is helpful to remember that the Annual Review is a legal requirement and serves the specific purpose of reviewing a child's Statement of Special Educational Needs. As such, it needs to focus on the information contained in the Statement in relation to needs, provision, teaching objectives, the child's and the parents' views. This is required for evaluation and decision making and does not need to go into the level of detail which can be included in a school report. At the secondary stage in particular, subject teachers may wish to comment in detail on the child's achievements in their subject area in the school report. This will not be necessary in an Annual Review report, except to indicate the level of the child's attainments, especially in a subject which is not causing concern and which is not a point of focus in the Statement. Similarly, while it may be important to comment at length in the Annual Review on, say, how a literacy problem is being addressed, this will be inappropriate in a school report.

When attempting to combine the information required for the Annual Review and school report, the task is often compromised. There is also the problem of timing. The school report is not normally required until the end of the year. The Annual Review report has to be produced on each anniversary of the statement. It may therefore be preferable, depending on which one is required first, to keep the processes separate but make clear to parents that the information will be used in both reports, as appropriate. For instance, if a school report produced in July contains valuable information about the child's attainments and needs in various areas, there is no reason why this should not be built upon for the purpose of the Annual Review if this is to follow in the Autumn term.

ANNUAL REVIEW REPORT (Specimen)

Name: Dan   Date of Birth 1.12.88

Address:
Names of Parents/Person responsible:
School: NC Year:
Class teacher/Tutor:
Date of Statement/Last Annual Review:
Date of Current Annual Review Meeting:

Details of existing provision from (a) school (b) LEA (c) other agencies:

Please list those invited to the Annual Review Meeting. Please indicate with an (A) those who attended, any reasons given for non-attendance, and tick who provided written contributions.

Name   *Position/Relationship*   *Additional Information*

1. *Previously Identified Needs*
(a) Special Educational Needs: from Statement/last Annual Review

1. Language difficulties, particularly in respect of verbal communication skills.
2. Weak literacy skills, especially writing and spelling.
3. Weak numeracy skills, especially number operations.
4. Low confidence and self-esteem.
5. Weak study skills.
6. Weak motor skills.

(b) Non-educational needs: from Statement/last Annual Review
    1. Asthmatic – problems with school attendance due to poor health.

(c) Overall objectives from Statement/last Annual Review
To enable Dan to improve:
    1. Language and communication skills.
    2. Reading and writing development.
    3. Numeracy development.
    4. Confidence and self-esteem.
    5. Study skills.
    6. Motor skills.

(d) Targets set and worked towards since Statement issued/last Annual Review (see section 1(a) Special Educational Needs)
    1.1: Encourage Dan to contribute to small group/class discussion.
    1.2: Improve listening and attention skills to ensure improved comprehension and retention of key information.
    2.1: Improve reading accuracy, reading comprehension, reading fluency and speed, by approximately 6 to 9 months.
    3.1: Develop number competence through mastery of the four rules of number.
    3.2: Encourage and improve use of calculator.
    3.3: Develop understanding and competence with fractions and decimals.
    4.1: Enable Dan to have regular, planned opportunities for success in his work and to give him feedback on a daily basis.
    4.2: Encourage Dan to participate in group work which is planned in such a way as to make him feel listened to and valued.
    5.1: Improve concentration and attention skills through structured tasks, systematically planned and implemented.
    5.2: Encourage Dan to actively extract information in his reading and discussions, to make notes, and record his work for future reference.
    5.3: Help make a structured and realistic time plan for study during school hours.
    6.1: Improve hand/eye coordination and, more specifically, encourage the development of
        – fine motor and coordination skills, including threading, throwing, aiming and catching skills;
        – handwriting through the development of a cursive script.

2. Report on Progress over Last Year
(a) Strengths
    1. Excellent auditory short term memory.
    2. Developing handwriting.
    3. Gaining confidence in all aspects of school life.

4. Enthusiastic.
5. Able to share feelings and experiences with a group.
6. Polite, well-mannered and displays good behaviour.

(b) Extent to which objectives outlined in 1(c) and targets set in 1(b) have been met:

1. Language and communication skills

Dan now speaks confidently in front of a group, whether taking a part in a play or presenting a poem. He has a much improved vocabulary and is able to communicate his thoughts effectively and with clarity.

2. Reading and writing development

Dan has made gains of approximately six months in respect of reading and spelling accuracy. Reading comprehension is also much improved, as is legibility and speed of writing.

3. Numeracy development

Dan has made progress across the curriculum, most recently in Maths AT2 'number' and mental calculation.

4. Confidence and self-esteem

Dan has settled well at R L School, making several friends and becoming a popular class member. He has responded to the small, structured and supportive environment where he has been able to experience success in a number of areas, both in his social relationships and with the curriculum.

5. Study skills

Dan is interested and works consistently in all subject areas. He shows good application to his work and is keen to improve and succeed. He is to be encouraged to:

– Improve his concentration span from 10 to 15 minutes.
– Improve his speed of work, including its presentation.
– Demonstrate more originality and creativity in his writing.
– Identify and extract the key issues in dealing with different types of information.
– Develop effective strategies to improve his access to the curriculum.

6. Motor skills

The PE programme and practical subject areas provide Dan with opportunities to develop his motor skills. These will be used to improve:

– Fine motor skills, e.g. hand/eye coordination, manipulative skills.
– Gross motor skills, including balance, physical agility, spatial awareness.

(c) Factors identified as affecting the achievement of objectives (i.e. significant change in the pupil's circumstances)

Dan's attendance at school is now much improved, following the change in his medication to control his asthma. His circumstances are also more settled at home, so he is generally happier and more able to devote time to his studies. His older brother, with whom he used to share a room, has moved out and he can now work quietly and without interruption in the evenings and weekends.

3. National Curriculum

(a) Teacher assessment of profiles of the current levels of attainment in the National Curriculum core subjects

Subject	Level Achieved	Level Working On
English		
Speaking and listening	2	2/3
Reading	2	2/3
Writing	1	2
Spelling	1	2
Handwriting	1	2
Mathematics		
Using and applying	2	3
Number	2	3
Algebra	2	3
Measure	2	3
Shape and space	2	3
Handling data	2	3
Overall levels experienced in Science		
Scientific investigations	2	3
Life and living processes	2	3
Materials and their processes	2	3
Physical processes	2	3

(b) Details of any modifications, disapplications or arrangements made to deliver a broad and balanced curriculum

> It has been possible to deliver the full National Curriculum through a systematic, differentiated teaching approach within small groups of no more than fouteen.

(c) Extent to which the National Curriculum, or any arrangements substituted for the National Curriculum, has been effective

> Dan has been achieving at around Level 2 of the National Curriculum in the core areas (see detailed breakdown). The relevant Attainment Targets have been broken down into small steps, taught within a systematic, sequential approach, with the emphasis on overlearning and skill consolidation.

4. Special Educational Needs

(a) New needs which were not recorded on the Statement

> Dan shows some artistic ability and talent and is to be entered for GCSE.

(b) Needs recorded on the Statement which are no longer present

> Speech and language difficulties as recorded on Statement are not such severe weaknesses and no longer call for speech therapy.

(c) Summary of current special educational needs in the light of the Review: Special Educational Needs

      1. Moderate learning difficulties.
      2. Language, literacy and numeracy difficulties.
      3. Physical and coordination problems.

(d) Summary of current non-educational needs in the light of the Review

      1. Asthma – which is now well controlled by medication.

5. *Recommendations for the coming year*
      Specific targets for the coming year:

(a) Short term objectives

      Dan will

      1. Make oral presentations for at least 2 minutes and up to 5 minutes.
      2. Participate in silent reading and group reading for a total of 20 minutes daily.
      3. Further improve the legibility and speed of his handwriting.
      4. Engage in selected maths activities and use a calculator when appropriate.
      5. Engage in estimating and checking tasks of increasing difficulty.
      6. Succeed in the tasks he is allocated, at least 50 per cent of the time, to maintain his enthusiasm and build on his confidence.
      7. Maintain high standards in attendance and thought for others.

(b) Long term objectives

      1. Improved language and communication skills, as shown in clarity, confidence and competence in his communications.
      2. Greater independence with learning and other tasks as assessed on agreed measures between him and his teacher.
      3. Achieve full potential in curriculum areas and in particular to:
         – develop basic literacy and numeracy skills, with improvements of between 6 to 9 months in a school year;
         – attain Level 3 of the National Curriculum in the core areas in the coming year.
      4. Achieve at least Grade C in his Art GCSE.
      5. Undertake vocational training and experience for two weeks, full time.
      6. Be offered an appropriate post-16 placement.

(c) How will the provision available be used to meet these targets?

      1. Small teaching groups.
      2. Supportive, structured teaching/learning environment.
      3. Differentiated work and materials.
      4. Individual programmes, tackling recognised weaknesses.

(d) How will the non-educational provision available be used to meet these targets?

      None specifically allocated. However, some support will be offered in order to help with attendance and confidence building.

(e) Any additional National Curriculum arrangements including any modifications or disapplication of the National Curriculum. In the case of disapplication the provision proposed to be substituted to maintain a broad and balanced curriculum
> None

6. Pupil's views
> Dan feels that he has made consistent progress in his work and is particularly pleased with his Art work. He would like to have continuing help with literacy and is keen to take books home to practise his reading skills.
>
> This has been a good year for Dan. He feels healthier and more able to maintain regular attendance at school. He is also more able to participate in physical activities and is gaining confidence all round. Dan says he is very happy in school, having made many friends with his teachers and his peers.

7. Views of Parents/Person Responsible
> Mr and Mrs G are pleased that Dan is so well settled in school. They are relieved that his medication seems to be controlling his asthma and feel sure that his more regular attendance will enable him to sustain progress. Both parents are now able to spend time with Dan and help him with his work without distraction.

8. Conclusions and Recommendations to the LEA
> Have the pupil's needs changed significantly since the last Annual Review?   Yes/No
>
> Is a change in the level or nature of educational/non-educational provision recommended?   Yes/No
>
> Is the pupil's current placement inappropriate for the coming year?
>   Yes/No
>
> If the answer to any of the above questions is 'Yes', please specify the amendment to the Statement you are recommending. Make reference to attached reports which support your recommendation.
>
> Does a Statement need to be maintained?   Yes/No
>
> If the answer is 'No', you are recommending that the LEA ceases to maintain the Statement. It is important, therefore, that there is evidence that this has been fully discussed at the Annual Review meeting.

Proposed date of next Annual Review Meeting:

Report prepared by: (please print)

Head teacher's signature: Date:

9 Year 9 Reviews and Transition Plans

The 1981 Education Act required the reassessment of children's special educational needs as they approached Year 9 of their schooling. The 1993 Education Act abolished this requirement. Statutory reassessments at age 13½ to 14½ were replaced with Year 9 Reviews which had to incorporate the preparation of Transition Plans. As Annual Reviews are required every year, the Year 9 Reviews effectively became two reviews, carried out in tandem. The first follows the usual Annual Review format. The second focuses on the steps necessary to enable young people to make an effective transition from school to adulthood. These are incorporated in a Transition Plan that has to be produced within one week of the Review meeting.

The revised Code introduces a new service known as the Connexions Service which has the task of working with schools to prepare, monitor and implement the Transition Plan. This service is expected to ensure that a team of personal advisers are working with young people in order to help them progress into training, employment or some form of learning, by removing barriers to their participation. Personal advisers attend Transition Plan meetings, work on building trust with young people, advocate on their behalf and generally provide advice, guidance and personal support to help them to prepare for their adult working life and to reach their potential. They undertake assessments and work with statutory and voluntary agencies to ensure that the needs of young people are met. These are key roles that could have an impact on young people's futures and personal advisers must therefore have an understanding of the issues young people face in transition to adulthood. The Connexions Service has a wide-ranging responsibility to work in partnership with young people and to empower them to play productive roles in schools, colleges and the wider community. The aim is to help them to participate as active citizens, with access to all the opportunities and facilities to which they are entitled, facilitating their social inclusion. Connexions will have a key role in removing barriers to their participation, and in dealing with risks of disaffection and disengagement in learning, vocational training or employment. This is a considerable challenge on a new service and Connexions will engage a wide range of agencies to meet young people's transition requirements, especially at the initial stages. Personal advisers may be found within schools, LEAs, Health and Social Services. In schools, consideration may be given to SENCOs or other teachers undertaking this role, such as designated teachers for looked-after children. In local authorities, youth workers, educational psychologists, welfare officers and social workers are also able to act as personal advisers. They may all undertake the short training of around ten days in the first instance so that they may develop the required awareness of the personal adviser role. Some may wish to proceed to the part-time Diploma for Personal Advisers, currently proposed to be spread over ten months.

It will be important to recognise that personal advisers will not necessarily be a distinct group of practitioners to be provided by the Connexions Service; they may come from a range of statutory and voluntary services working in partnership with each other though they will be identified as undertaking the role of personal adviser. Year 9 Reviews and transition planning is only a small element of the work expected from Connexions and this will require SEN experience and expertise. The major task, however, will be to engage all young people and to prevent the risk of their disaffection from school or society.

The purpose of the Transition Plan

The Transition Plan is intended to be a comprehensive document compiled to enable the smooth transition of the young person from school to adult life. It spans the final years of schooling and can be conveniently divided into the following time frames:

1. The final two years of schooling, i.e. 14 to 16.
2. The years following transfer from school to college, training or employment, i.e. 16 to 19.
3. Transfer to higher education, further training or continuing employment, i.e. 19 to 21.
4. The 'adult' years, especially when the person needs support with independence, employment or the active involvement and support of Social Services, e.g. with respect to care plans or funding for care arrangements.

Consequently, it is important that the Transition Plan is regularly reviewed and updated to ensure that the needs identified and issues raised are kept in focus and remain under active consideration. This will not happen unless proposals are clearly defined and tasks are clearly agreed and allocated, with arrangements built in to monitor progress, check on outstanding issues and trigger action. This will require liaising with and involving relevant parties at all stages, i.e. not only at the time of the 14+ Review but at all subsequent reviews and planning meetings.

The Transition Plan should therefore include an action plan which clearly specifies the action required, the people responsible and the time frames being worked to. Transition planning is a continuous and evolving process and indicators will be helpful to monitor performance and measure progress over time. A Transition Plan is not a static document that can be finalised at Year 9; it should be continually adjusted to ensure that it is taking account of the young person's changing needs and aspirations. The Code suggests that the transition planning process should be 'participative, holistic, supportive, evolving, inclusive and collaborative' (DfES 2001a, p. 131).

The tasks of schools in relation to Year 9 Reviews and Transition Plan meetings

The key tasks for schools are to discharge their obligations as specified in the young person's Statement of Special Educational Needs, in addition to the objectives agreed at the 14+ Review. They should activate the Transition Plan and keep the action agreed under regular review. They should also work closely with the Connexions Service and with other key agencies such as the LEA, Social Services Departments and the Careers Service.

Schools provide a central point of reference and contact to outside agencies until such time as some other agency takes over. They should check that plans are being followed; if not, they should alert personal advisers so that together they may chase up whoever is responsible for action. Their contact with the young person enables them to fulfil an informed and supportive role and they can work in partnership with parents to promote the young person's best interests.

The role of statutory agencies

The LEA

The LEA *must* organise the 14+ Review and invite the personal adviser who can work with the school in preparing the Transition Plan from information which is factual and accurate and which presents the young person in a positive light. Within two weeks of the start of the school year the LEA must, through the Connexions Service, provide information to the personal advisers about all young people in their area who require a Year 9 Review. Schools must inform Social Services of the date of the meeting and the school leaving date for a young person who is considered disabled. Schools should also invite the personal adviser and Careers Service to future reviews and ensure that the Learning Skills Council is informed of any special arrangements. It may only pass on information to relevant parties with the consent of the young persons and their parents.

The revised Code sets out the requirements for young people with Statements of SEN but only provides brief details about other children who may experience difficulties in learning but who do not have Statements. The latter group should not be excluded from the transition planning process if this is appropriate and it is likely that personal advisers will take a lead role in this so that young people are able to access the facilities they require.

The Code also makes reference to Section 140 of the Learning Skills Council Act 2000; this refers to an assessment that may be required for some young people. This assessment should look forward and build on information that is already available. Looking back and attempting to criticise previous provision is not the intention. Neither should there be need for new assessments for children with or without SEN as a wealth of documentation should already be available, e.g. professional reports, school reports, IEPs; statements and annual reviews. New Section 140 assessments should only be required where the young peron's needs have changed or if there is a significant change in their circumstances and agencies with current or previous involvement should be consulted.

The Social Services Department

The Social Services Department *must* carry out a multi-disciplinary assessment and produce care plans for children and adults experiencing significant special needs; make arrangements for people over 18 years of age if they have required help from the department prior to their eighteenth birthday; and give the young person choice on whether to accept or refuse assessment and help under the terms of the Disabled Person's Act 1986.

The role of professional advisers

Professional advisers include those employed by the LEA or statutory agencies, e.g. educational psychologists, doctors, careers advisers and social workers. They can also be engaged by parents and are not restricted to those currently involved as others may be called in as the need arises.

Their main tasks are to determine the young person's needs; help formulate the Plan without pre-empting the action; accept responsibilities which are within and not outside their remit and facilitate the consultation and meeting process. Their main role is to provide advice on professional issues within their expertise.

A checklist of the issues to be addressed, including an action list for this group, is provided in Appendix 8.

How to prepare a Transition Plan

The original Code of Practice provided guidance on the questions to be addressed in the preparation of a Transition Plan. These are broken down into four sections dealing with the role of the school; the responsibilities and contributions of professionals; the expectations and involvement of parents and the hopes, aspirations and needs of the young person.

The questions

The questions included in the original Code of Practice are reproduced below. These have been omitted in the revised version as they appear elsewhere in the SEN Toolkit (DfES 2001b). They provide a very helpful frame of reference and guidance. Schools may wish to use them to help with their preparation of Transition Plans.

The school
What are the young person's curriculum needs during transition? How can the curriculum help the young person to play his role in the community; make use of leisure and recreational facilities; assume new roles in the family; develop new educational and vocational skills?

The professionals
Which new professionals need to be involved in planning for transition: for example, occupational psychologists, a rehabilitation medicine specialist, occupational and other therapists? How can they develop close working relationships with colleagues in other agencies to ensure effective and coherent plans for the young person in transition? Does the young person have any special health or welfare needs which will require planning and support from Health and Social Services now or in the future?

Are assessment arrangements for transition clear, relevant and shared between all agencies concerned? How can information best be transferred from children's to adult services to ensure a smooth transitional arrangement? Where a young person requires a particular technological aid, do the arrangements for transition include appropriate training and arrangements for securing technological support? Is education after the age of 16 appropriate, and if so, at school or at a college of further education?

The family
What do parents expect of their son's or daughter's adult life? What can they contribute in terms of helping their child develop personal and social skills and an adult life style and acquire new skills? Will parents experience new care needs and require practical help in terms of aids, adaptations or general support during these years?

The young person
What information do young people need in order to make informed choices? What local arrangements exist to provide advocacy and advice if required? How can young people be encouraged to contribute to their own Transition Plan and make positive decisions about the future? If young people are living away from home or attending a residential school outside their own LEA, are there special issues relating to the location of services when they leave school which should be discussed in planning? What are the young person's hopes and aspirations for the future, and how can these be met?

Responding to the questions

The school
What are the young person's curriculum needs during transition? This question is more easily answered by reference to the Year 9 Annual Review and after

discussion has taken place with young people and their parents on their proposals for the future. The important point relates to young people's needs during transition, i.e. at 14+, which represents the final two years in school and before transfer to further education. The emphasis, therefore, depends on the priorities and objectives agreed at the 14+ Review. Consideration also needs to be given to the following:

1. Given the time available, which skills or subject areas are to be given priority while at the same time providing a broadly based, balanced curriculum?
2. How does the curriculum prepare the young person for transition and how relevant is it to the options to be pursued at 16+?

If the young person's intentions for the future are known, identifying the curriculum needs is fairly straightforward. For instance, a disabled 14-year-old who is keen on a career in television or journalism would probably find the inclusion of word processing, dictating and communication skills in the curriculum to be useful preparation and training. Similarly, an able-bodied 14-year-old with aspirations to enter engineering would do better to include technical and science subjects in his course of study. The key is to ascertain in which direction the young person is heading. This, combined with an assessment of his strengths and weaknesses, together with an evaluation of the career opportunities likely to be open to the young person, should facilitate and guide planning of the curriculum areas which require emphasis and coverage at this stage of education. New 'skills gaps' may be identified, or long-standing weaknesses may require remediation. The provision of compensatory strategies may also need to be considered for weaknesses which are particularly resistant to teaching and improvement.

The curricular emphasis will depend on the long-term aim for the young person. If it is considered that he should continue in further education and be prepared for employment, then work and vocational skills will be a priority. These could include the development of timekeeping, self-organisation, punctuality, presentation and communication skills. On the other hand, if the aim is to encourage independence, then the curriculum should focus more on life skills, e.g. self-care, budgeting and shopping, menu planning and preparation and self-advocacy.

Action 1

1. Consult with young person and the parents.
2. Determine career aspirations and future plans.
3. Agree curricular priorities and additions for final two years at school.

How can the curriculum help the young person to play his role in the community? The information required will relate to the skills the young person will need so as to play a meaningful and productive role in the community. For some students, this could mean development of vocational and work related skills. For others, it could mean no more than the development of life and independence skills, perhaps relating to self-care, mobility or social skills.

Action 2

1. Determine role young person is likely to play in community, e.g. employment prospects and levels of independence achievable.
2. Plan curriculum and include the teaching of skills which would be a useful preparation for transition to adult life.
3. Explore community options, such as work experience, and provide opportunities to practise skills *in situ.*

How can the curriculum help the young person make use of leisure and recreational facilities? Teachers would have already established the young person's leisure and recreational interests. It is also likely that a full programme of activities is already provided at school, which can be easily extended in the wider community. For example, a young person may be actively involved in the school's sporting activities and these could easily continue as future leisure and recreational pursuits, the facilities and arrangements having already been made available. An understanding of the opportunities young people will benefit from in the long term will be helpful and these could quite easily focus on specific aspects of their development, e.g. physical, aesthetic, spiritual, personal or social development.

Action 3

1. Determine young person's recreational and leisure interests and review opportunities offered by school.
2. Extend and consolidate on recreational and leisure pursuits of long-term interest or significance.
3. Make and develop links between young person, parents and leisure provider.
4. Determine and agree objectives and include in Transition Plan.

How can the curriculum help the young person to assume new roles in the family? This may not always be necessary. Many parents might feel that their teenager is already playing a full part and this would need to be recognised and acknowledged. Where this is not so, consultation with children and their parents will be required to determine how and in which areas new roles are relevant and achievable. It may be that for some young persons this new role will involve assuming greater responsibility and independence for themselves or greater involvement in family activities, and this would need to be carefully ascertained with a view to determining the order of priority.

Action 4

1. Seek the views of parents and, with the young person, agree role expected or that is appropriate within family setting.
2. Define this role and how it is to be supported.
3. Establish how progress is to be reviewed and future plans made.

How can the curriculum help the young person to develop new educational and vocational skills? This has already been touched upon in this chapter under the guidance on the young person's curriculum needs during transition. New educational skills relate to future requirements and current interests. A person who wishes to enter the world of travel and tourism might wish to undertake a serious study of languages. This would represent an addition of both educational and vocational skills. On the other hand, someone interested in commerce may opt for business studies and possibly learn vocational skills such as the use of computers for word processing and the production of spreadsheets and databases. The key is to identify young people's career aspirations and match these to their educational requirements.

Action 5

1. Identify skills necessary for or linked with career choice.
2. Establish most appropriate route or course for student to follow on leaving school.
3. Prepare for this within the curriculum.

The professionals
Which new professionals need to be involved in planning for transition: for example, occupational psychologists, a rehabilitation medicine specialist, occupational and other therapists? This would of course depend on the young person's special needs. Occupational psychologists are likely to be helpful in matching career choice to abilities, needs and aptitude and will be able to advise on the appropriateness or otherwise of some career aspirations. Rehabilitation medicine specialists will be needed for advice regarding children who have clear medical and physical needs, i.e. those continuing to require extensive medical care, including further surgery. For example, some young people may require revision of medical and other aids, e.g. for hearing, vision or mobility. Others may need continuing support with regard to chronic problems, e.g. dialysis for kidney dysfunction or failure, corrective treatment for deformities. These will require specialist medical advice and support, especially if young people have to be moved from their home area for further education.

Occupational therapists are invaluable in the provision of advice relating to children who experience physical difficulties, especially with regard to the adaptation of learning material or in the living accomodation itself. They work closely with Social Services and can act as an important link between school and this agency. Other therapists include physiotherapists whose role remains central to the support of children experiencing severe physical difficulties.

Schools may find that it is difficult to ensure the attendance of some of these specialists, in which case they should liaise with a representative of the department concerned, e.g. the Clinical Medical Officer for the rehabilitation medicine specialist and the physiotherapist, the educational psychologist for the occupational psychologist, and the social worker for the occupational therapist.

Action 6

1. Decide who needs to be involved.
2. Establish contact, if not already done, and name agency.

How can they develop close working relationships with colleagues in other agencies to ensure effective and coherent plans for the young person in transition? In the majority of cases, this is likely to be through contact with the school at planning and Annual Review meetings. If tasks are allocated to named parties for action and follow up, this will be one way of ensuring that communication is started and continued with the parties who require to be involved. Plans, however, will only become effective and coherent after consultation, discussion and agreement to fulfil the agreed priorities identified.

Action 7

1. The relevant agency will decide how to do this.
2. School may volunteer to be the point of contact.

Does the young person have any special health or welfare needs which will require planning and support from Health and Social Services now or in the future? This is especially important for children with medical or social needs, including those who require sheltered accommodation, and unable to lead a completely independent life. Advance warning of their requirements should normally have taken place within the assessment required of the Social Services Department at 14+ under the terms of the Disabled Persons Act 1986. This will help provide the necessary information and alert the relevant parties to current and future requirements.

Action 8

1. Establish requirements with Health or Social Services.
2. Record these and name contacts for follow up and action.
3. If young person is disabled, seek the views and assessment of Social Services under the Disabled Persons Act 1986.

Are assessment arrangements for transition clear, relevant and shared between all agencies concerned? Until the young person leaves school, this will be the responsibility of the school, working closely with careers advisers and other agencies.

Action 9

1. Agree who is going to take lead responsibility for this.
2. Name this agency.
3. Build in monitoring and review arrangements through meetings to determine progress and action required to achieve plan.

How can information best be transferred from children's to adult services to ensure a smooth transitional arrangement? Normally, this would be done through the transfer of school records, preceded by regular communication at meetings through prior involvement of the agencies providing adult services.

Action 10

1. Transfer school records at the appropriate time.
2. Ensure planning requirements are undertaken well beforehand and that agencies are alerted sufficiently early.

Where a young person requires a particular technological aid, do the arrangements for transition include appropriate training and arrangements for securing technological support? An example of this would be a communication aid for children with no speech, activated through a computer. Other examples include visual and mobility aids, in which case the appropriate specialists, e.g. mobility officers, would need to be involved.

Action 11

1. Establish whose responsibility it is to provide and fund the equipment or service.
2. Make contact with and remind parties of equipment/service needing to be in place at the time of student's transfer, if not earlier.

Is education after the age of 16 appropriate, and if so, at school or at a college of further education? This would depend on a number of factors including the current placement and facilities available. Other factors will relate to the type of course, curricular and other experiences. It is likely that a great deal of this information will be directly available from the Annual Review.

Action 12

1. Weigh up all available options and discuss 'pros and cons' with all parties.
2. Agree most appropriate option and consult with service provider, i.e. LEA or Learning Skills Council (LSC).
3. If additional costs are likely to be incurred, alert service providers in plenty of time.

The family
What do parents expect of their son's or daughter's adult life? Parents will require some help and guidance with this question. A suggested simplification is:

– What do they consider to be their child's medium to long term needs?
– What skills would they like him to develop?

– What kind of experiences are they seeking for him?
– What are their priorities in terms of preparing their child for an independent, meaningful and productive future?

Parents will be well advised to consult with their son or daughter when answering this question.

What can they contribute in terms of helping their child develop personal and social skills, an adult life style and acquire new skills? Again, this may need to be simplified to ensure parents answer all three questions. They may need examples and discussion beforehand.

Will parents experience new care needs and require practical help in terms of aids, adaptations or general support during these years? This relates mainly to children who experience extensive needs such as severe learning or physical difficulties. It will be important for parents to be advised to be tactful in the use of any labels they might need to use to define their child's needs.

Action 13

1. Provide simplified questionnaire to parents in advance of meeting.
2. Help and advise as required
3. Include or revise information in the light of discussion at meeting, following full consultation with and agreement of parents.

The young person
What information do young people need in order to make informed choices? This can only be established following careful consultation and discussion with the young person. This is likely to be done by the teacher responsible for careers in the school, working closely with the personal adviser. They will take their lead from the student and explore options on the young person's behalf, followed by the provision of specific information on the career choices available. This information will probably include a range of suitable courses in FE colleges locally, work employment opportunities, or vocational training schemes.

This information is usually in print but may need to be modified to ensure the student has full access. Help with discussion and to ensure understanding of the content of the information may also be needed.

Action 14

1. Arrange for information to be available at school.
2. Organise meeting with specialist for student if possible.
3. Record outcome of discussions and proposals.

What local arrangements exist to provide advocacy and advice if required? The LEA should already have published information on these sources with regard to the statutory assessment procedures. This should be used for the purpose of reference. Alternatively, the voluntary agencies provide a good source.

Action 15

1. Make available within school information on sources for advocacy.
2. Develop contacts with these agencies and include them in discussion and planning where this is acceptable to the student and parents.

How can young people be encouraged to contribute to their own Transition Plan and make positive decisions about the future? This would normally involve extensive preparation by teachers whom the student trusts and can work with. Parents would have also been party to these preliminary discussions and consultations. The main requirement is that students are able to make informed choices through knowing the options available and those to which they are best suited. Some may not be able to do this on their own, either because of communication difficulties, a lack of understanding of the issues involved, or lack of confidence. This is when they will require strong advocacy, based on insight of their needs and aspirations.

Action 16

1. Explain purpose of Transition Plan.
2. Talk this through so that student understands and can contribute.
3. Provide the fullest information possible.
4. Talk through the 'pros and cons' and determine student's preferences.
5. Provide opportunity for discussion with specialists, e.g. careers adviser.
6. Record discussions and communicate proposals at meeting.
7. Prepare and empower student at meeting.

If young people are living away from home or attending a residential school outside their own LEA, are there special issues relating to the location of services when they leave school which should be discussed in planning? This is especially pertinent to the student returning to the home area, requiring a period of retraining and readjustment to suit their new circumstances. There are issues here for the visually impaired person in particular who may require mobility training, or for the physically disabled whose living accommodation may need to be adapted well in advance. Similarly, individuals with significant medical needs requiring specialist medical help would need to have these agencies alerted beforehand.

Action 17

1. Make contact with 'home' authorities.
2. Determine local circumstances and services from these sources.
3. Alert agencies to requirements through clear specification of student's needs.
4. Do not pre-empt local decision making; local agencies know their services and circumstances best.
5. If procedures need to be explained to student and parents, do so or refer them to the most informed party.

What are the young person's hopes and aspirations for the future, and how can these be met? This is the crucial question which can only be answered from extensive knowledge of the young person. Sometimes it is simple enough for teachers to determine his hopes and aspirations, especially if they have been in regular contact with the student and know about his needs, abilities, interests and aptitudes. Some of these may have already been communicated by the student. However, there are instances when teachers, in consultation with parents and other parties, have to determine future choices but this should never be done without firsthand knowledge and teaching of the young person.

Action 18

1. Meet with student and his parents.
2. Consider profile of attainments, expressed interests, strengths, weaknesses, demonstrable talents.
3. Determine career aspirations through consultation and discussion with all concerned parties.
4. Consider match between abilities and interests, and aspirations.
5. Discuss and agree action.

TRANSITION PLAN (Specimen)

This Plan should be completed at the Annual Review meeting for a young person in Year 9 and above and should be attached to the Annual Review Report.

Name: Thomas D   Date of Birth: 10.6.88
Address:
Names of Parents/Person Responsible:
School: NC   Year: 9
Date of Current Annual Review Report (attached):
Expected school leaving date:

School perspective

1. Summary of likely curriculum needs up to 18th year and new educational and vocational skills to be developed:
(a) Development of numeracy and literacy, including money, budgeting, time and social sight vocabulary.
(b) Development of interpersonal and social skills, e.g. presentation skills, communication, group discussion/collaboration/cooperation, relationships and responsibilities.
(c) Development of life and independence skills, e.g. preparing for work, adult life.

New skills to be developed:
Educational. Link between work and curriculum experiences, specifically citizenship skills, e.g. development of personal autonomy, creative and independent thinking, decision making.
Vocational. Preparation for training in car maintenance, e.g. timekeeping, practical experience.

2. How will the curriculum help the young person to play a role in the community, make use of leisure and recreational facilities and assume new roles within the family?
(a) Community Care module will provide Tom with opportunities to work with other people: the elderly, children, the physically frail or disabled.
(b) Opportunities to extend learning into the community through Link Courses, Citizenship, PSE, Work Studies.
(c) Provision of opportunities to take part in leisure and recreation activities, e.g. skiing, sailing and canoeing, in addition to traditional games and PE as available locally.
(d) Develop Tom's awareness of his changing role and responsibilities, including personal, social and financial elements.

People involved

1. Which new professionals need to be involved in planning for transition, e.g. occupational psychologists, the careers service, rehabilitation medicine specialist, occupational and other therapists, representatives from the local college?

(a) Specialist Careers Adviser.

(b) Representatives from specialist courses in local colleges/training agencies (New Horizon).

2. How can they develop close working relationships with colleagues in other agencies to ensure effective and coherent plans for the young person in transition?

(a) Careers Adviser to meet with Tom and his parents to explore suitable post-16 options within the full range available.

(b) Careers Adviser to organise visits/placements once opportunities have been identified and agreed, and to liaise with all parties, including parents.

(c) Representatives to attend relevant meetings at RE school and specify their requirements.

3. Does the young person have any special health or welfare needs which will require planning and support from Health and Social Services now or in the future?

Housing/accommodation is likely to be a requirement at 19+ and will need to be planned for at an early stage.

4. Are assessment arrangements for transition clear, relevant and shared between all agencies concerned?

Information will be available from RE School based on the outcome of Tom's individual experiences. His individual experiences will be evaluated and information integrated within Annual Reviews. He will, however, benefit from assessment by the Training Agency or other relevant body that might become appropriate at the time.

5. How can information best be transferred from children's to adult services to ensure a smooth transitional arrangement?

(a) Pre-transfer meetings and regular liaison.

(b) Full documentation will be sent to receiving agency as soon as transfer identified and agreed.

(c) Use of networking agencies, such as Careers Advisers.

6. Where a young person requires a particular technological aid, do the arrangements for transition include appropriate training and arrangements for securing technological support?

Tom will require continued access to an Archimedes computer or, alternatively, retraining in the use of a personal computer. Relevant software to include word processing with a spellcheck will also be needed.

Family views

1. What do you expect for your child in adult life?
(a) Employment within the car maintenance trade.
(b) Housing/accommodation at 19+.

2. How can you help your child develop personal and social skills and an adult life style and acquire new skills?
(a) Through encouragement, advice and support.
(b) Help to develop his interests and encouragement to attend youth clubs and other groups.
(c) Increasing responsibility to manage his affairs, particularly money.
(d) Help with transition from education to work, e.g. help with applications, interviews, transport.
(e) Support with his training requirements.

3. Will you experience new care needs and require practical help in terms of aids, adaptation or general support during these years?
No.

Young person's views about future educational needs

1. On the job training.
2. Continuing help with literacy and numeracy.

Young person's needs

1.   Information requirements:
(a) Post-16 options (leaflets and preferably videos).
(b) Careers software for special needs children.

2.   Contact points for advocacy and advice:
(a) RE School.
(b) Careers advice (Tel:).

3.   In helping the young person contribute to the Transition Plan, guidance and support have been offered by:
(a) Class teacher.
(b) Head of Upper School.

4.   Local services, contact names and addresses:
(a) Careers (Tel:).
(b) College (Tel:).

Please list those who contributed to the Transition Plan:

Names   *Position/Relationship*

Signature: Date: Position:

(A copy of the Transition Plan is being circulated to all those who are being sent the Annual Review Report.)

10 Parents and the Code of Practice, and SEN Tribunals

Introduction

The Code of Practice is a comprehensive document, representing an extremely useful source of reference for parents and other parties. It details parental rights and expectations and gives parents and their children a voice on how help should be planned and provided in schools. The Code reinforces key principles and values, some established and enshrined in legislation. These include an increased emphasis on the rights of children and the recognition that their development and welfare are of paramount importance (Children Act 1989). The rights of parents to be active and equal partners in supporting children experiencing special educational needs are further reinforced. The responsibilities of parents towards their child's need to receive regular and efficient education remain as they were under the Education Act 1944. The responsibilities and accountability of schools, in particular, receive greater emphasis; these are made explicit under School Action and School Action Plus. The duties of LEAs to provide services to help them work in partnership with parents are expanded to require the provision of independent mediation.

Responsibilities of schools towards parents

The Code requires that schools publish their Special Educational Needs Policies (see Chapter 4), which are to be made available to parents and are to be reviewed annually so that they may be evaluated. These policies must detail the arrangements which operate within the school to identify, assess and provide for children experiencing difficulties in learning, together with the names of persons who will act as points of contact for parents.

Schools are expected to follow a graduated approach to assessing and providing for children experiencing special educational needs, involving parents at every stage. This includes full consultation with the parents and their active involvement from the time their child is identified as experiencing a learning difficulty. The objective is to ensure that parents are able to become equal and active partners, playing a full part in supporting their child. They must be told of any educational provision or intervention proposed.

Schools must keep IEPs and other records which are shared with parents and to which they contribute. They must organise regular meetings and reviews with parents at which IEPs can be reviewed in terms of progress achieved, targets set and future action and planning. They must also advise parents of their child's needs and progress and guide them through School Action and School Action Plus, up to and beyond the completion of statutory assessment.

Schools have to organise Annual Reviews for children who are provided with a Statement of Special Educational Needs, ensuring the necessary liaison and consultation on behalf of the LEA.

Responsibilities of schools towards children

The Code requires schools to consult with children and to ensure that their feelings and views are represented regarding any planning undertaken on their behalf. They must ensure that children, where they are able, are encouraged to play an active role and to be fully involved, including their attendance at meetings. Pupil participation is significantly reinforced in the revised Code and now forms a separate chapter, reflecting the importance placed upon it. It is particularly appropriate in target setting, planning IEPs or Group IEPs and is essential with children who are either undergoing or have undergone the statutory assessment process. Pupil views should be recorded and should feature routinely in all reports, e.g. educational psychology and Annual Review reports.

Roles and responsibilities of parents

The main legal requirement is that parents ensure that their children receive regular and efficient education (1944 Education Act). An extension of this is the role played by parents in safeguarding the best interests of their child. This is mainly arrived at through advocacy, based on an understanding of children's and parents' rights, including the efficient discharge of the duties and responsibilities undertaken by parents.

The Code makes provision for parents to act as advocates for their child. This is achieved by means of requirements placed on other parties towards the parents and their children as consumers of the service they receive. The 'duty of care', however, applies to all parties in respect of the assessment procedures, particularly those defined by law, i.e. the statutory multi-professional assessment.

Parents have to be especially careful that they understand and are able to exercise their rights at various stages of their child's statutory assessment. In particular, parents are well advised to understand the processes and systems which apply at the stages preceding statutory assessment, i.e. School Action and School Action Plus. They need to know about the kinds of planning, teaching and documentation required of schools. This is in order to be able to evaluate these against the Code's recommendations and is particularly important if their child is likely to require statutory assessment. They need to know if schools have indeed exhausted all the options in terms of teaching and provision from within their internal resources. This is because this will have a direct implication on the LEA's response regarding requests for statutory assessment. LEAs are unlikely to agree to undertake statutory assessment unless they are satisfied that exceptional arrangements and resources are required which are beyond the ability of the school to provide. As 90 per cent of resources are expected to be delegated to schools by 2003–04, there should be decreasing needs for statutory assessment. LEAs will also be wanting to evaluate the quality and intensity of the educational intervention, together with the reliability and validity of the documentation and evidence.

Parents' statutory rights

Under the 1996 Education Act, parents have the right to request a statutory assessment if they are concerned about their child's learning difficulties. The LEA will need to consider the request and provide the parents with a written decision within six weeks. The LEA will normally have to comply, unless this is considered to be unnecessary.

Parents may refuse to have their child assessed if he is under two years of age, and may make representations against statutory assessment if they consider this to be unnecessary or premature. They have a right to consider their responses to proposals for statutory assessment, whether or not initiated by themselves or others acting on their behalf. They have a statutory period of 29 days within which to make their views known to the LEA. They may submit their own advice as the 'Parental Advice' to their child's statutory assessment. This will include their assessment of their child as parents, the child's strengths and weaknesses and the help that is needed.

Parents may also submit 'Parental Representations', which are advice prepared for them by a professional, friend or adviser working on their behalf. In any event, such advice must be submitted within 29 days, starting from the date of the LEA's proposal letter to carry out the statutory assessment.

Parents must receive a copy of the LEA's proposed Statement of Special Educational Needs for their child, if one is to be issued within 18 weeks of the start of the statutory assessment procedures. Alternatively, they should receive a 'Note in Lieu' of a Statement if one is not to be issued following completion of the statutory assessment, within a time limit of 18 weeks. A Note in Lieu will specify the reasons why a Statement is not to be issued, including the consultation available if parents are dissatisfied with such an outcome. They should receive a copy of the final, 'signed' Statement within 26 weeks of the date when statutory assessment was started. They may respond and comment on the proposed Statement of Special Educational Needs within 15 days of its receipt and either confirm their agreement to it or raise their concerns. In the latter case, they may request a meeting with an LEA officer, again within 15 days. Two further meetings can also be arranged if the matter cannot be resolved but parents need to request these within 15 days of each preceding meeting.

Parents can expect to be guided through the statutory assessment process by an officer of the LEA. This person is to act as their point of contact with the LEA, to answer queries, give advice and generally help parents with the procedure and requirements. They should also be advised of a person who is independent of the LEA and who can act as a friend and adviser in respect of the statutory assessment. The revised Code also entitles them to have information on mediation and conciliation services and this must be provided by the LEA.

Parents may state a preference for a school unless this is unsuitable for their child's education, incompatible with the education of the majority of the children already at the school or represents ineffective use of resources from the point of view of the LEA. They may appeal to an independent Special Educational Needs Tribunal if they are unable to agree with the LEA's assessment.

Parents must be invited to Annual Reviews of their child's Statement and must be consulted and involved in the preparation of the Transition Plan at the Year 9 Annual Reviews for children aged 14+.

Statutory time limits

This diagram sets out the statutory time limits in respect of statutory assessment.

LEA considers whether or not to initiate statutory assessment procedures: *6 weeks. (This usually follows a request from a parent or a recommendation from school or other agency)*

LEA carries out the statutory assessment: *10 weeks. (This is for the seeking and collection of the necessary advice)*

LEA decides whether or not to make a Statement of Special Educational Needs: *2 weeks (LEA's options are to make a Statement or to issue a Note in Lieu)*

LEA finalises the Statement: *8 weeks. (This 8 week period starts from the date the LEA serves the proposed Statement, ending with the date on which the Statement is finalised)*

Exceptions to time limits

The time limit of 26 weeks is waived if the following conditions apply:

- the child and parents are absent from the area for longer than four weeks;
- the LEA is aware of exceptional personal circumstances affecting the child or his parents during the assessment period, e.g. illness, family bereavement;
- the LEA requests advice from a head teacher relating to the request for statutory assessment during a period beginning one week before the school closes for a continuous period of not less than four weeks and ending one week before it is due to re-open;
- parents are late in their submission of their advice or evidence by six weeks or more dating from the time of the LEA's request to them for such information;
- the child is not known to the local Health or Social Services Department;
- parents fail to attend appointments with any of the agencies involved in the statutory assessment;
- the parents are unable to agree the proposed Statement and seek more than one consultation meeting with an LEA officer to resolve matters;
- the LEA seeks further advice following receipt of all the appendices normally required for the Statement; this may be for the purpose of clarifying issues, seeking further specialist advice or any follow up action the LEA believes to be necessary;
- the LEA requests educational advice during a period beginning one week before the school closes for a continuous period of not less than four weeks and ending one week before it is due to re-open;
- the LEA needs to seek approval to use an independent school and is unable to obtain a decision from the DfES within two weeks.

These exceptions to the statutory time limits apply at various stages of the assessment period. Some apply to the initial six week period when the LEA is considering its response to requests for statutory assessment. Others are specific to the ten week period which follows when the decision is made to proceed with the assessment. The first three exceptions in the above list apply to the former, the rest are more specific to the ten week time limit within which the LEA must make an assessment.

Action for parents

Parents should observe the time limits which apply to all the stages of the statutory assessment procedure. They may request to see IEPs and other records which have been prepared in response to their child's special educational needs. They should ask for clarification of any of the proposals that are unclear to them, and expect to be involved in supporting, monitoring and reviewing their child's progress. They should liaise closely with their child's school and be guided by its advice on what has been done, what is being done and what needs to be done in the future.

Parents may request help, advice and guidance either from the LEA or from the adviser if they have a query at any stage of the assessment process. They should make their views known to all parties including the LEA, and query any advice or recommendations which appear to diverge from or to contradict advice or recommendations offered by others. It will be helpful for parents to seek explanations and justifications from all professionals involved in order to evaluate the rationale and validity of the advice. It is important to avoid confusion and misunderstandings, which can later lead to disagreement or dispute, and thereby obviate a need for formal hearings at Special Educational Needs Tribunals where differences of view will be subject to close scrutiny to determine which is the more valid. Crucially, parents would wish to be actively involved in all aspects of planning relating to their child's education.

The role of parents in statutory assessments and Annual Reviews

Parents have a role to play at all stages, including those preceding the decision for statutory assessment to be made. It is important that they involve themselves at School Action and School Action Plus, i.e. the school based stages of the Code when much valuable and preventative work can be done to deal with children's special needs. They should consult and work closely with their child's teacher or Special Educational Needs Coordinator, supporting initiatives and proposals, activating teaching plans and strategies, and engaging in reviews to determine the progress being made.

Parents do not need to be teachers to make an active contribution to their child's education. There are a number of areas where they, as parents, have a natural and distinct advantage. They have the major role with regard to the encouragement and development of self-help, communication, social and life skills which are used every day in the context of the home. Studies have shown that parents can and do make a difference in these areas (see Macbeth 1989). They can also work in partnership with teachers to help in the teaching and consolidation of a number of skills, e.g. the teaching of reading through 'shared approaches' where the emphasis is on the child and the parents sharing and enjoying the activity. 'Shared reading' constitutes quality family time and involvement for the young child. For the older child in secondary schools, 'paired reading', where child and parent take it in turn to read, has been shown to be effective (see Tizard *et al.* 1982, Tizard and Hughes 1984, Topping and Wolfendale 1985, Branston and Provis 1986). Similarly, shared writing has been shown to be effective (see Hannavy 1995).

Parents should therefore be looking at every opportunity to support their child, especially if it is with regard to an activity that they can be confident about sharing and enjoying with their child. However, if this should cause them any worry or anxiety which is likely to be transmitted either consciously or unconsciously, they should avoid becoming involved, leaving the task to teachers and support staff.

Providing advice for statutory assessment

At the stage when the LEA decides to initiate statutory assessment procedures, parents are invited to contribute to the assessment through the provision of written advice. They can prepare this advice themselves or they can seek the help of others, probably a professional adviser, to make written representations on their behalf. The intention is to give them the opportunity to advise the LEA of their child's special educational needs and how these should be met.

Wolfendale (1988) provides some useful guidelines on the parental contribution to assessment and these have been adopted in the Code of Practice. Essentially, they cover parental observations and concerns about both the past and the current situation, together with the parents' recommendations for the future.

Parents might wish to consider using the following checklist in the preparation of their advice for submission to the LEA in respect of statutory assessment. This has been adapted from Wolfendale, taking account of developments from the Code of Practice.

The past
1. What can you remember about the early years, in terms of your child's development?
2. Were there any problems with the pregnancy, at or after birth?
3. Did anything else of significance happen?
4. When did you start feeling that things were not right? Was your child perhaps slow in sitting up, walking or talking? Was he 'too good' as a baby, 'too placid, never cried'? Did he want attention? Did he respond to it? Did he show any interest in being picked up? Was he a cuddly baby?
5. How did he compare with other children of his age? Did he seem to be behind, perhaps in his speech or his play? Did you worry about his hearing or other aspects of his development? What help did you receive?

The current situation
1. What are your child's strengths, i.e. what is he particularly good at?
2. What are his weaknesses and how could he be helped with these?
3. What are his likes and dislikes? In particular, what should teachers and others be aware of during the school day, to encourage his involvement and minimise the risk of causing him anxiety or distress? Does he have any particular interests that could be used in teaching?
4. How are you helping your child at home? What aspects of this work has been influenced, guided and supported by teachers? Do you feel this is making any difference or would you advise on a change of emphasis in any area?
5. What have been your contributions at meetings in school to review your child's progress? Do you believe anything else should be tried?
6. What is your child's perspective about his current situation? How is he viewed by his siblings or his peers?

Special educational needs
1. What do you consider to be your child's most significant needs? Could you list these in priority order? For example, if it is speech, should 'listening'

skills be dealt with first, comprehension of simple instructions second and expression and articulation of words third? Do you have any advice on what could be stopping your child from making progress?
2. How long have you been aware of your child's special educational needs? What has been done about these?
3. How is your child dealing with his learning difficulties? Does he feel he is getting the right support? What other help would he like or benefit from?

The future: both immediate and long term
1. What should happen now; at home and at school? What is needed immediately?
2. What are your main worries and concerns?
3. What is the best way of helping? Has this been tried before and should anything be done differently this time?
4. Who is the best person to help and how frequently should the help be provided?
5. How is your child's progress going to be monitored, i.e. how would you and your child's teacher know that he is making the intended progress?
6. How long would you be waiting between progress meetings or reviews?
7. Is the help that you are looking for immediately available in your child's school? Describe the arrangements you would wish for your child. What is his view about the future?

A photocopiable version of the above checklist is included in Appendix 6.

Parents' advice for Annual Reviews

Parents have a right to contribute advice, both written and verbal, in respect of Annual Reviews. Written advice is required, by law, of schools and the LEA and is an option for parents of which they should take advantage.

In preparing their advice, parents may find the following helpful. They may also wish to refer to the 'Agenda for Parents at Annual Reviews' which is covered in Chapter 8 of this book.

Special educational needs: the past
1. What does the Statement say about the child's special educational needs? Is this still accurate?
2. How have the special educational needs in the Statement been addressed? What has worked? What has not worked so well? What remains to be done and how?
3. Observations on the teaching arrangements/strategies. What has been effective or not so effective and how should changes and improvements be made?
4. In relation to targets set, how many have been achieved? Which are proving hard to deal with and what else is required? Is there evidence of progress, if not, why not?

The present and future

1. What are the priorities for the coming year? What is the best way of achieving these, in the light of past experience?
2. What help would the child/the parents/the school need?
3. Are there concerns about the curriculum? What are they? How could these be addressed and what are the legal constraints, e.g. specific curricular requirements at key stages such as the need for a modern foreign language at secondary stage.
4. What are the contingency arrangements in the event of proposals and plans needing to be dropped/changed? What should be the process in terms of consultation, parents' involvement? This is particularly important, especially if the parents themselves decide to initiate changes.

The child's perspective

1. How does the child feel about the past year? What achievements has he made and what are the challenges that he wants to undertake?
2. What are his priorities and how do these fit in with his own plans/aspirations for the future?
3. Is he comfortable with all the arrangements, e.g. staff, resources, physical arrangements, pace of learning, expectations, level of support?
4. How does he view himself in comparison with his peers? What help does he need?

A version of the above checklist is included in Appendix 7.

What can parents expect of their LEAs?

Parents can expect their LEAs to provide information relating to the statutory assessment procedures. This should be made available in a number of languages in order to be accessible to parents to whom English is a second language. LEAs may also provide interpreters when this is needed. Guidance must also be provided during and throughout the statutory assessment procedures and the parents should be informed on progress, when required. This is normally the responsibility of an officer of the LEA. LEAs are expected to deal with parents' requests and queries in respect of statutory assessment promptly and effectively, within the specified time limit which applies at each stage of the process. The revised Code emphasises the importance of parents being provided with details of Parent Partnership Services; these should have an independent element which is particularly valuable in the event of conflict or dispute between parties over any aspect of the statutory assessment process.

Parents as education partners?

The Code makes it clear that parents should be seen as partners in the education of their child. They have a wealth of firsthand experience and expertise which ought to be tapped by teachers and others, if a thorough understanding of the whole child and their circumstances is to be achieved. Parents can provide information relating to the level and degree of support they can make available at home, and the resource that they represent to teachers and children should not be underestimated.

Education is a continuous, lifelong process and parents are the active educators for the majority of the time each day, albeit not always necessarily working on the same curricula. Research suggests that when these do coincide with the school's priorities there are effective and beneficial outcomes all round, examples being parental partnership in shared reading schemes and portage.

Special Educational Needs Tribunals

There will be occasions when, in spite of the best endeavours, parents and their LEAs are unable to agree on the best course of action. This is why Special Educational Needs Tribunals (SENT) came into being. The Tribunal is an independent body, led by a legally qualified chairman, first set up under the 1993 Education Act to determine appeals by parents against LEA decisions on assessments and Statements. It replaces the appeal committees that existed before implementation of the 1993 Education Act. These were staffed by teams of local authority councillors and could only make recommendations to the LEA which could choose to ignore them, leaving appeal to the Secretary of State as the only recourse open to parents. Their impartiality was also questioned as councillors were perceived as protective of the LEA's interests.

The Tribunals, on the other hand, make decisions which are binding on both parties to the appeal. They were intended to bring consistency, fairness and expertise to appeals, but risk become threatening and legalistic.

Parents can appeal to the Tribunal if they are unhappy with their LEA's decision. There are six grounds. The first is when the LEA refuses to assess their child, following a request from them or from school. The second is when the LEA refuses to issue a Statement on completion of the statutory assessment. The third arises when the LEA issues a Statement but parents are unhappy with the contents; they may appeal against any part of the Statement, except for Parts 5 and 6; e.g. the LEA's description in Part 2 of the child's special educational needs; the special education provision described in Part 3 and the school named in Part 4 or the failure to name a school. The fourth ground is where LEAs refuse to change the named school at which a child is placed. The fifth and sixth grounds for appeal arise when the LEA decides to cease to maintain an existing Statement and when it refuses to carry out a statutory re-assessment.

The revised Code does not require the naming of a school in Part 4 in all cases; therefore in this section LEAs may describe the type of school which can appropriately meet the child's needs. Parents, however, have to appeal within two months of receiving the LEA decision, using a signed Notice of Appeal form. If the Tribunal decides that the appeal is within its remit, the following timetable applies. The whole process, between parents lodging an appeal and the Tribunal hearing, is not expected to take longer than four or five months.

Tribunal decisions are not given on the day of the hearing; they are sent to parents and the LEA normally within ten working days. These confirm whether the Tribunal is upholding or dismissing the appeal. Details are provided on the facts of the case, the Tribunal's rationale and their decision.

Special Educational Needs Tribunal: Timetable

1. Parents appeal within two months of receiving LEA decision.

2. Tribunal sends 'Appeal Notice' to LEA within 10 working days.

3. LEA has to confirm its response within 20 working days, i.e. whether or not to resist the appeal and on what grounds. Parents may provide further information in respect of their appeal within this time period.

4. Tribunal sends LEA's response to parents, this being at the time of receipt.

5. Tribunal sends forms to LEA and parents, requesting details of how they are to be represented at the hearing. Forms are required to be returned by a stated date.

6. Parties notified of date, time and place of hearing at least 10 working days beforehand.

7. Written notification of Tribunal decision within 10 working days of hearing.

Issues outside the remit of Tribunals

Special Educational Needs Tribunals have no power to deal with parental complaints about the way a school is providing for a child's needs, or failing to do so; the length of time the LEA takes to assess or provide a Statement for a child; or the way in which the LEA conducts the assessment. The way in which the LEA describes the child's non-educational needs in Part 5 and the manner in which it intends to provide for them in Part 6 are also outside of its remit.

Tribunals are not involved in testing how LEAs arrange the help specified in the statement.

In these cases, parents may direct their concerns to any of a range of agencies. Each of these will have varying powers of redress. In the first instance, parents may approach the governing body of the school, the LEA, or elected members in their area. Alternatively, they may take up their concerns with the local Member of Parliament. In the event of serious complaints, they may ask the Local Government Ombudsman to investigate, especially if they feel that there has been maladministration and that they or their child are at risk of being caused an injustice. They may also seek a judicial review through the High Court. Who the parents approach will depend on the nature of their complaint and the channel most appropriate to deal with this in relation to their powers of jurisdiction. If there is a simpler and more easily accessible remedy, this would be the route to follow; for example, the High Court is likely to be reluctant to consider issues which are more appropriately dealt with at an SEN Tribunal. Similarly, the Local Government Ombudsman would wish to know that mechanisms for local resolution of complaints have been exhausted before agreeing to investigate. Most authorities have their own complaints procedures and these should be explored. However, no party should ever lose sight of the advantages of resolving matters locally and every opportunity should be used to make this happen.

Costs

A Tribunal will not normally award costs, except in exceptional circumstances, if, in its view, either party is acting frivolously, vexatiously or wholly unreasonably. Legal aid is not available for Tribunals but can be available to the child in respect of judicial review, though some of the initial legal costs are not covered.

SEN Tribunal: statistics

Since the SEN Tribunal was set up in September 1994, there have been over 11,000 cases registered, with administrative costs of around £3 million per annum (SENT 2000). The President's yearly reports detail the nature and range of activities undertaken; these also confirm the types of special educational needs where arbitration are commonly required. Table 10.1 illustrates this. These figures exclude the costs of appeals to the High Court in respect of SEN Tribunal decisions at around 50 cases per year, totalling around 300 by year 2000. Most Tribunal appeals have been in respect of specific learning difficulties, autism and challenging behaviour and health therapies. Recently, there has been an increase in respect of children experiencing speech and language difficulties. Table 10.2 shows the distribution for the period 1995–2000.

Table 10.1 Number of appeals registered with the SEN Tribunal 1994–2000 (SENT 2000)

Year	1994/5	1995/6	1996/7	1997/8	1998/9	1999/2000
Number	1,161	1,626	2,051	2,191	2,412	2,463

Table 10.2 Types of appeals heard at the SEN Tribunal 1995–2000: Number (Percentages in brackets) (SENT 1996–7, 1997–8, 1999–2000)

Type of SEN	1994/5	1995/6	1996/7	1997/8	1998/9	1999/2000
Autism	(3)	(4.2)	123(6)	240(11)	313(13)	319(13)
Emotional and Behavioural Difficulties	(6)	(7.3)	140(6.8)	204(9.3)	272(11.3)	315(12.8)
Epilepsy	(1)	(1)	15(0.7)	17(0.8)	23(1)	31(1.3)
Hearing impairment	(4)	(2.5)	63(3.1)	64(2.9)	73(3)	75(3)
Literacy (including SpLD)	(40)	(39.6)	745(36.3)	783(35.7)	818(33.9)	932(37.8)
Moderate learning difficulties	(9)	(11.1)	189(9.2)	161(7.3)	153(6.3)	142(5.8)
Multi-sensory impairment		(0.2)	3(0.2)	6(0.3)	4(0.2)	4(0.2)
Physical handicap	(5)	(4.2)	124(6)	132(6)	142(5.9)	124(5)
Severe learning difficulties	(6)	(6.2)	87(4.2)	74(3.4)	91(3.8)	75(3)
Speech and language problems	(9)	(8.4)	186(9.1)	199(9.1)	287(11.9)	274(11.1)
Visual impairment	(1)	(0.9)	27(1.4)	28(1.3)	31(1.3)	31(1.3)
Other/Unknown	(16)	(14.4)	349(17)	283(12.9)	205(8.5)	141(5.7)
Total appeals registered (1161) (242 heard)	(100)	(100)	2,051(100)	2,191(100)	2,412(100)	2,463(100)

How to prepare for SEN Tribunals

Before the SEN Tribunal (SENT), it is helpful to anticipate and to comply with time limits. The timescale is tight for both parties. Once the reports are circulated by the tribunal, they should be carefully studied. This helps to identify areas where there is common ground as well as the issues where there may be discrepancy, divergence and disagreement. A list of these points, together with clear references (e.g. page and paragraph numbers), saves time at the Tribunal and can help with presenting a logical, reasoned and well structured argument in support of a point of view.

It may be helpful to address some questions and to have answers prepared before the hearing; it is most important to know what the appeal is about; what the parents want and why the LEA is unwilling to comply with their request. Clarity of role is crucial, as well as the ability to defend a position or particular point of view. The way in which advice is given orally or in writing also needs to be considered. There are inevitable challenges to expect from the other parties, including the Tribunal panel. Statements should be made clearly and some points will require further clarification at the hearing; therefore risks and pitfalls should be identified beforehand so as to be avoided or overcome.

Parties will need to identify the issues for the LEA, the parents, the SEN Tribunal and themselves. Strategies which may help deal with problematic situations are to avoid jargon, not to get drawn into conflict and, if unsure, to ask the chairperson for guidance. It is important always to address the chair and not be put off by reactions from the other side. These may be quite deliberate in an attempt to cause ridicule or confusion. It is also helpful to be brief and concise, to make key points, and if possible say how many points you are presenting. A list of each and every special educational need experienced by the child will be required, including information on how they should be met. Children are occasionally in attendance for part of the hearing so care must be exercised to ensure that their views are heard and that they are not caused any avoidable distress. Parties should not speak to members of the Tribunal panel after the hearing, especially if they are known to them; in one case this was alleged to have caused prejudice in a Tribunal's decision (see Ramjhun 1995).

The style of Tribunals is changing to becoming more informal and more conducive to open and productive discussions between opposing parties (SENT 1994/5). Aldridge (1995), as President of the SEN Tribunal, confirms that Tribunals are likely to favour the approach which promotes the child's best interests, as opposed to sitting in judgement on the LEA's decision-making process. He suggests that they will be looking at all the evidence on which the LEA's original decision is based, including new information which is considered relevant to the child's needs.

Some final comments

The Code of Practice has been welcomed in many quarters as representing a significant milestone in furthering the cause of children experiencing special educational needs (Bowers 1996). It provides, as it sets out to do, clear, detailed and practical guidance relating to how children are to be supported in schools, including the procedures, processes and systems to be followed, thereby building in efficiencies and accountabilities.

The Code itself provides a structure for all schools and if followed has the potential to lead to many benefits. These include planned, active and systematic consultation and the involvement of children and their parents in how they are helped with their education; a clearer appreciation of children's entitlement and parental rights and expectations and detailed guidance for all parties relating to the requirements of the 1996 Education Act. It also expects schools to describe their policies, procedures and practices on how they meet the needs of children experiencing special educational needs. A graduated approach to assessment, planning and provision is encouraged and guidance given on the preparation of IEPs, the conducting of Annual Reviews and the preparation of Transition Plans. Public reporting of schools' implementation of their Special Educational Needs Policies increases transparency. There are also increased efficiencies and accountabilities, particularly from LEA staff with regard to statutory assessment and Annual Reviews (see also Millward and Skidmore 1998).

However, as with other legislative initiatives, the Code has its critics. Among the concerns raised are the increased bureaucracy that may result from its implementation, especially in the absence of increased resources. The additional workload on teachers, and SEN Coordinators in particular, has also been a cause for concern (see, for instance, Bowers *et al.* 1998). This derives from the planning and support they are expected to provide in a sytematic and accountable way, in addition to the increased requirements for formal consultation between teachers, children, parents and other parties.

There are fears about raising expectations of some parties, e.g. parents and pressure groups who may find in appeals a route through which to further their own cause (Gross 1996). Appeals also provide opportunities for the growth and expansion of professional groups, particularly among educational psychologists and other specialists who have found an increased demand for their services as expert witnesses either for parents or for the LEA. Parallel with this has been the increasing involvement of the legal profession. While it was rare for lawyers to be involved in education in the 1980s, this situation seems to be fast changing.

There are also continuing concerns from LEAs about the impact of Tribunals and how this affects their ability to work within limited, finite resources. Tribunal appeals inevitably cause uncertainty to all parties and their decisions can have serious funding implications, especially to smaller LEAs with tight budgets. Though the revised Code requires Tribunals to have regard to LEA policies and practices, their focus remains on the needs of the individual child. This risks cutting across the needs of other children (Gross 1996). However, the task of balancing the needs of the individual with those of others remains with LEAs.

A continuing increase in confrontation, disputes and appeals seems inevitable, especially with the introduction of the 2001 SEN and Disability Discrimination Act. Schools and local authorities will need to be prepared to devote time and energy to increased legal challenges; while increasing the rights of individuals at risk of being oppressed should be applauded, moving education into the legal arena is likely to prove costly. A deplorable consequence would be if professional groups involved in litigation are the only ones to prosper at cost to the public good. What is certain is that less resources will be available in schools for children as more funds are directed towards defending appeals or other litigation. SEN Tribunal costs are already substantial; the new SEN and Disability Tribunals (SENDISTs) will cost even more. Can these be afforded? That SENDISTs have required to be created speaks volumes about the society we are in and the sad fact that disability discrimination is considered in such urgent need of legal resolution.

This is a reflection on society and on its need to change (Armstrong *et al.* 2000). It is also symptomatic of the increasing drive towards the rights model in education as elsewhere (Faupel 1994). The recognition of disability rights (see Oliver 1990) is here to stay; with this comes the valuing of diversity and the removal of barriers to social participation and inclusion. A focus on individual rights must not, however, completely lose sight of the collective good. LEAs are required to provide 'efficient education', not 'the best education', though this is without doubt everybody's aspiration. Can they really afford to differentiate the provision made according to every child's needs or rights? LEAs can only aspire to achieve efficient education; higher ideals are probably neither realistic nor affordable, not just in this country but worldwide.

Gross (1996) illustrates the potential dilemmas in LEAs' allocation of resources in asking whether current educational legislation should be reshaped to end resource allocation based on individual needs or whether the solution is to increase individual advocacy in the pursuit of rights. Such advocacy should be equally accessible to all parents, irrespective of social class or educational background, empowering them to advocate effectively for their children. This might overcome the risks of advocacy based systems of resource allocation to favour 'the adult articulate and politically aware sections of the community' (Macready 1991). Riddell *et al.* (1999) have shown that parental and organisational advocacy can divert resources away from some children in favour of others; in their study, the beneficiaries were children experiencing specific learning difficulties. Gross (1996) also illustrates this argument in respect of integration, e.g. an increasing number of children with a diagnosis of Down's syndrome are in mainstream education while those experiencing emotional and behavioural difficulties are being excluded (Hayden 1997). Bald (1995) suggests that the former group were enjoying the greatest rise in integration; 80 per cent were in mainstream education and this percentage is rising. The benefits of their inclusion are also atttracting increasing research support (see Buckley 2000). While positive moves to reduce discrimination are to be applauded, I believe that the key word in education should now be realism and the need to move gradually and sensibly towards increasing individual rights. It is recognised that the pursuit of the collective good or collective rights has been perceived as a means of promoting oppression, especially in the disability literature (see Oliver 1990). There is no excuse for oppression; however, the way forward is to plan sensitively and on secure foundations, to enable the participation of all without one individual's needs and rights conflicting with those of others. It is to be hoped that SENDISTs will make sure that there are more gainers than losers.

At the time the original Code was introduced in 1995, the DFE believed that its implementation would be cost neutral in schools. They expected that schools would already be following the model of practice offered, providing a structured approach to meeting children's special educational needs. However, it was soon clear that this was not the case. Audits carried out in Cambridge LEA suggested the breakdowns shown in Table 10.3 regarding additional workloads generated at each stage of the Code, per child.

Table 10.3 Additional workload

Stage of original Code of Practice	Hours
Stage 1	4.9
Stage 2	5.2
Stage 3	6
Stage 4	2
Stage 5	7

Johnson (1995) quantified this as requiring 878 hours, i.e. 0.9 of a whole teacher equivalent, in an 11–16 comprehensive school of 1,000 children. This was based on an estimate derived from audits carried out in Kent and Lambeth LEAs that the percentages of children shown in Table 10.4 will require help at each of the stages.

Table 10.4 Percentage of children requiring help

Stage	Percentage
Stage 1	7
Stage 2	4
Stage 3	5
Stages 4 and 5	2

In a more recent study, Bowers *et al.* (1998) found that most SENCOs estimated that they spent around eight hours per week on administrative activities related to the original Code. However, non-contact time to enable them to do this work varied markedly between primary and secondary SENCOs; the former had significantly less time. On average, primary SENCOs had 1 hour 40 minutes, while their secondary counterparts received around 4 hours 25 minutes.

There continue to be concerns in schools and LEAs on how to fund the requirements. The revised Code accepts that there are time implications for schools, and SENCOs in particular. Removing the need for detailed IEPs or for an SEN register might help. Reducing expectations from schools in relation to their submissions for statutory assessment may further serve to reduce bureaucracy. However, there may be risks that as the number of Statements is reduced and more emphasis is placed on IEPs accountability may not be so transparent or easily measured. This is because of continuing concerns about IEPs being seen by some as simply a form-filling exercise (see Cooper 1996). Though advocated as a cornerstone of Public Law 94–142 in the United States where IEPs were intended to unite educators, parents and students in a team effort to achieve an appropriate education for students experiencing difficulties in learning (Lovitt *et al.* 1994), there are risks when IEPs are not used effectively. These have been demonstrated by studies in the United States. Sigafoos *et al.* (1993) found that a relatively small amount of time was devoted to IEP targets, with the majority of pupils spending time on tasks not relevant to their IEPs. This lack of coherence between IEPs and classroom practice was also confirmed by Lynch and Beare (1990). However, the UK experience might be different in the light of schools' movements towards self reviews and within the framework of LEA and Ofsted inspections. These might hold the key to quality assurance. It would be a tremendous achievement if parents could have the confidence that IEPs are likely to make a greater difference to children's learning than Statements or other statutory procedures. IEPs which are effectively implemented will obviate the need for Statements and may replace the chasing of resources that statutory assessments have caused; they provide a more appropriate and effective approach to making a difference to children's learning (Marsh 1998, Ramjhun 2001). The revised Code was carefully written to promote best practice. If it succeeds in achieving consistency and a degree of uniformity in school practices for the majority of children experiencing difficulties in learning, then it should be judged a success. How it will fare, however, only time will tell.

Appendix 1

How to formulate and write a Special Educational Needs Policy

1. Agree school's mission statement or equivalent at Governors' meeting.

2. Use the mission statement to frame Special Educational Needs Policy.

3. Define Special Educational Needs Policy in the context of:
   - the school's ethos
   - the school's needs and objectives
   - the school's aspirations for all children
   - the governing body's values and principles
   - the children's entitlement
   - parents' rights and expectations.

4. Detail in priority order:
   - the principal objectives of the Special Educational Needs Policy
   - the arrangements to operate within school to support the Policy and, in particular, the financial and human resource arrangements.

5. Provide the names of key staff, including those of the Special Educational Needs Coordinator and the Responsible Person, who are to act as links with parents and outside agencies.

6. Describe how:
   - children's learning difficulties are to be identified
   - children are to be helped
   - children's progress is to be reviewed and evaluated.

7. Include information relating to:
   - any specialism available from school staff
   - expertise that can be called or bought in
   - special facilities, resources
   - means of enabling access to these facilities.

8. Include details of the procedures and processes to be followed in the event of:

   - a query
   - a complaint.

9. Describe the consultation and partnership arrangements with:

   - parents and other parties
   - statutory agencies.

10. Include information on how success in achieving the objectives of the Policy is to be evaluated and its form and frequency of reporting.

11. Include a summary of the Special Educational Needs Policy in the School Prospectus.

Appendix 2

(Appendices 2 and 3 contain two examples of other formats of Individual Education Plans, see Chapter 5)

Individual Education Plan (Example i)

Name:　　　　　　　Date of Birth:　　　　　　　Class:　　　　　　　Date completed:

Long term goal:

Date	Targets	Teaching Arrangements	Success Criteria	Date Start	Date Finish

Appendix 3

Individual Education Plan (Example ii)

Name: Date of Birth: Class: Date completed:

Date	Target	Environmental Change	New Skills	Reinforcement	Success Criteria

Appendix 4

(This Appendix is a Checklist of questions to ask at School Action of the Code of Practice, see Chapter 6)

School Action: Checklist

Name: **Date of Birth:**   **Year:**

Learning difficulties

What is now known about the child's learning difficulty?

What methods have been tried and which ones have been more successful?

Are there areas where practice could be improved?

Priority

What is the priority area for attention and remediation?

Does this need to be broken down into sub-areas so that manageable objectives can be set?

Teaching strategy

Why did children not respond to earlier arrangements?

Where are adjustments/revisions required?

Should the focus be more on the child's learning style or greater differentiation of the curriculum?

Should teaching be in even smaller steps?

Staffing arrangements

What staffing arrangements need to be made to provide the child with the help that he or she needs?

How will this help be secured, organised, monitored and evaluated?

Signed   **Designator (e.g. SENCO)   Date**

Appendix 5

(This Appendix is a Checklist of questions to ask at School Action Plus of the Code of Practice, see Chapter 6)

School Action Plus: Checklist

Nature of learning difficulty

Are the child's needs so complex as to require significantly more help and a different type of approach to that provided earlier?

Teaching and assessment

Have the teaching interventions been systematically planned and given sufficient time to work?

Have these been based on concrete evidence of assessment? Give details.

Which areas of the child's functioning seem to be more resistant to change?

Priorities for action and performance indicators

What are the priority areas to address?

What would serve as useful indicators to monitor and evaluate progress?

Concensus on learning difficulty

What is the consensus of opinion on the child's learning difficulty?

Does the child/parent/teacher/support staff feel that: (a) appropriate and (b) sufficient help has been given?

Consultation with teachers

Have all teachers been consulted? (It is essential in secondary schools to consult with teachers and establish their views. In which areas do they feel the child is doing well, which strategies are more likely to bear fruit?)

Consultation with parents

How do parents feel about the whole process?

Do they believe that they have been adequately consulted/involved?

Consultation with the child

How does the child feel?

Does the child understand and is he or she committed to the plan?

Does the child consider it realistic and what level of responsibility is he or she prepared/able to accept?

Standards setting and contingency planning

Have expectations and standards been clearly specified? Give details.

Which support structures are required to facilitate achievement of these?

What are the contingency arrangements to deal with problems, failures and unplanned events?

Appendix 6

(Parents might use this Checklist when preparing advice for submission to the LEA in respect of statutory assessment)

Parents' advice to statutory assessment: Checklist

The past
1. What can you remember about the early years, in terms of your child's development?
2. Were there any problems with the pregnancy, at or after birth?
3. Did anything else of significance happen?
4. When did you start feeling that things were not right? Was your child perhaps slow in sitting up, walking or talking? Was he 'too good' as a baby, 'too placid, never cried'? Did he want attention? Did he respond to it? Did he show any interest in being picked up? Was he a cuddly baby?
5. How did he compare with other children of his age? Did he seem to be behind, perhaps in his speech or his play? Did you worry about his hearing or other aspects of his development? What help did you receive?

The current situation
1. What are your child's strengths, i.e. what is he particularly good at?
2. What are his weaknesses and how could he be helped with these?
3. What are his likes and dislikes? In particular, what should teachers and others be aware of during the school day, to encourage his involvement and minimise the risk of causing him anxiety or distress? Does he have any particular interests that could be used in teaching?
4. How are you helping your child at home? What aspects of this work has been influenced, guided and supported by teachers? Do you feel this is making any difference or would you advise on a change of emphasis in any area?
5. What have been your contributions at meetings in school to review your child's progress? Do you believe anything else should be tried?
6. What is your child's perspective about his current situation? How is he viewed by his siblings or his peers?

Special educational needs

1. What do you consider to be your child's most significant needs? Could you list these in priority order? For example, if it is speech, should 'listening' skills be dealt with first, comprehension of simple instructions second and expression and articulation of words third? Do you have any advice on what could be stopping your child from making progress?

2. How long have you been aware of your child's special educational needs? What has been done about these?

3. How is your child dealing with his learning difficulties? Does he feel he is getting the right support? What other help would he like or benefit from?

The future: both immediate and long term

1. What should happen now, at home and at school? What is needed immediately?

2. What are your main worries and concerns?

3. What is the best way of helping? Has this been tried before and should anything be done differently this time?

4. Who is the best person to help and how frequently should the help be provided?

5. How is your child's progress going to be monitored, i.e. how would you and your child's teacher know that he is making the intended progress?

6. How long would you be waiting between progress meetings or reviews?

7. Is the help that you are looking for immediately available in your child's school? Describe the arrangements you would wish for your child. What is his view about the future?

Appendix 7

(Parents might use this Checklist when preparing advice for Annual Reviews)

Parents' advice to Annual Review: Checklist

Special educational needs: the past
1. What does the Statement say about the child's special educational needs? Is this still accurate?
2. How have the special educational needs in the Statement been addressed? What has worked? What has not worked so well? What remains to be done and how?
3. Observations on the teaching arrangements/strategies. What has been effective/not so effective and how should changes/improvements be made?
4. In relation to targets set, how many have been achieved? Which are proving hard to deal with and what else is required? Is there evidence of progress, if not, why not?

The present and the future
1. What are the priorities for the coming year? What is the best way of achieving these, in the light of past experience?
2. What help would the child/the parents/the school need?
3. Are there concerns about the curriculum? What are they? How could these be addressed and what are the legal constraints, e.g. specific curricular requirements at key stages such as the need for a modern foreign language at secondary stage.
4. What are the contingency arrangements in the event of proposals and plans needing to be dropped/changed? What should be the process in terms of consultation and parents' involvement? This is particularly important, especially if the parents themselves decide to initiate changes.

The child's perspective
1. How does the child feel about the past year? What achievements has he made and what are the challenges that he wants to undertake?
2. What are his priorities and how do these fit in with his own plans/aspirations for the future?
3. Is he comfortable with all the arrangements, e.g. staff, resources, physical arrangements, pace of learning, expectations, level of support?
4. How does he view himself in comparison with his peers? What help does he need?

Appendix 8

Action list for professional advisers at Transition Plan meetings

1. Come to the meeting prepared, i.e:
   Read the Statement
   Bring the file
   Make notes of the chronology of significant events
2. If time allows, produce a summary of the key issues in advance. This helps to focus the discussion.
3. Be clear about own role and do not make promises which cannot be kept.
4. Stick to areas of expertise. Do not stray into others.
5. Keep the focus on *needs*, not *provision*.
6. Make use of Records of Achievement, with consent.
7. Make notes at Transition Plan meeting to enable accuracy of record to be checked.
8. Ensure information is put together in a positive manner and presents young person in a positive light.
9. If you are responsible for producing the Transition Plan, make sure all parties are agreed on the records, especially the action.

Role of professional advisers: Issues to be addressed at the Transition Plan meeting

- Curriculum for the next two years and how this links into longer term plans
- Priorities for action:
    within *two* years
    at 16+
    Who does what, how, with what and by when?
- The young person's perspective
- The family's perspective
- Short, medium and long term plans for:
    the school
    others
- Essential links and the transition arrangements
- Legal requirements: Children Act 1989; Disabled Person's Act 1986; The National Health Service and Community Care Act 1990.

Glossary

Annual Review   A statutory meeting convened to review a child's Statement of Special Educational Needs. This considers the requirements of the Statement, reviews the steps taken to help the child and sets targets in terms of future teaching plans and action.

Appendix   This refers to the written submission of parents or the report of professional advisers in relation to a child's statutory assessment. Parents are invited to submit their advice or representation. Appendices are also routinely sought from teachers, doctors, educational psychologists and social workers.

Appendix A   This is the evidence submitted by the child's parents in connection with the statutory assessment. It constitutes the parental advice, written by or on behalf of parents to represent their views about their child's special educational needs.

Centile   This refers to the position achieved by a child in comparison with his peers. For example, a child who is at the 2nd centile in relation to his height is in the bottom 2 per cent for his age group as far as height is concerned. The same applies to reading or spelling, except that this would refer to his performance on a specific test, as compared with the performance of others in his age group.

Code of Practice   A guide to schools, Local Education Authorities (LEAs), Health and Social Services Departments about the help they can give to children experiencing special educational needs (SEN). Schools and LEAs must have regard to the Code in their dealings with children experiencing special needs.

Independent Parental Supporter   A person who is independent of the LEA and who provides information and advice to parents about the assessment procedures. This person can be a friend, relative or a member of a voluntary organisation.

Individual Education Plan (IEP)   A plan prepared by teachers in consultation with parents and others, to help children experiencing special educational needs. This should set out the nature of the learning difficulty, the action required and the strategies to be used, including the staffing arrangements to be made.

Learning Difficulties   A child has a learning difficulty if he or she finds it much harder to learn than most children of the same age.

124

Local Education Authority (LEA) Local government body responsible for providing education and for carrying out statutory assessments and maintaining Statements.

Note in Lieu of Statement A note issued by the LEA on completion of the statutory assessment. This is provided instead of a Statement and should normally set out the reasons why a Statement has not been issued.

Parent The word 'parent' in this book refers to any adult who exercises parental responsibility for the child, whether a natural parent or not, or who has care of the child. This adopts the definition as laid down in the Children Act 1989 to which the reader is referred for more details.

Parental Representation This is advice prepared by a professional adviser, on behalf of parents in respect of the statutory assessment of their child's special educational needs.

Professional Adviser Professional advisers are likely to have a background in teaching or educational psychology, i.e. with experience and expertise in SEN. They may also have a legal background but their main qualification would be that the parents have trust and confidence in their ability to act as their representative and to advocate on their behalf. The revised Code of Practice requires LEAs to provide Parent Partnership services with an independent element. These services are additional sources of professional advice and support to parents.

Proposed Statement of Special Educational Needs The LEA's proposed Statement of Special Educational Needs. It is unsigned and undated but contains all the advice submitted during the assessment procedure. The proposed Statement is only a proposal and a consultation document and has no legal validity. It cannot be appealed against, until it is finalised, i.e. until after it is signed and dated by a duly authorised officer of the LEA.

Responsible Person A Governor, acting on behalf of the governing body, or head teacher, who undertakes responsibility for discharging the school's Special Educational Needs Policy. This person must be kept informed about children's special educational needs and will ensure that teachers are aware of children who have been issued with a Statement of Special Educational Needs and their responsibilities towards them.

SEN Coordinator A teacher who has responsibility for coordinating special needs within their school.

Special Educational Needs (SEN) A child experiences special educational needs if he or she has learning difficulties calling for special educational provision.

Special Educational Needs Tribunal An independent body that hears appeals against decisions made by LEAs. It has a legally qualified chairman and two other 'lay' members, one with experience in the special needs field. Its decisions are binding on parties involved in the appeal.

Special Educational Provision The special help given to children experiencing special educational needs.

Statement of Special Educational Needs A legal document which sets out a child's needs and the extra help to be provided. This is in six parts.

- Part 1 is the introduction and lists biographical and other details, e.g. religion, home address, names of parents/guardians.
- Part 2 details the special educational needs as identified from the statutory assessment.
- Part 3 describes the Special Educational Provision to be made, including the teaching objectives and arrangements necessary to provide for the child's special needs.
- Part 4 names the type of school or other educational placement to be made.
- Part 5 describes any non-educational needs the child experiences, e.g. he may be asthmatic or epileptic or may require to be looked after by the Social Services, i.e. his needs are not strictly educational and are to be provided by a body other than the LEA.
- Part 6 specifies the non-educational provision to meet the child's non-educational needs, e.g. physiotherapy, speech therapy or help from the Social Services.

With the Statement, the Appendices, which are the reports provided by contributors to the assessment, will be attached.

Statutory Assessment   A very detailed examination of a child's special educational needs, undertaken by the LEA and carried out by a variety of professionals, including teachers, doctors and educational psychologists.

Talking Pendown   A voice synthesizer embedded in a word processor to help children with the development of their literacy skills. The computer 'talks' to the child, giving him instant feedback on the words that he is working with. (See *Archimedes Talking Pendown: Software and Guide Book*, published by Longman Logotron, 1993.)

Transition Plan   A plan drawn up at the first Annual Review after a child's fourteenth birthday. It sets out the steps and action needed to help the young person move from school to adult life.

Useful addresses

Action for Sick Children, Argyle House, 29–31 Euston Road, London NW1 2SD.

Advisory Centre for Education, 18 Aberdeen Studios, 22 Highbury Grove, London N5 2EA.

AFASIC – Overcoming Speech Impairments, 347 Central Market, Smithfield, London EC1A 9NH.

Association for Brain Damaged Children, 47 Northumberland Road, Coventry CV1 3AP.

Association for Spina Bifida and Hydrocephalus, Ashbah House, 42 Park Road, Peterborough PE1 2UQ.

British Diabetic Association, 10 Queen Anne Street, London W1M 0BD.

British Dyslexia Association, 98 London Road, Reading RG1 5AU.

British Epilepsy Association, New Anstey House, Gate Way Drive, Leeds LS19 7XY.

British Sports Association for the Disabled, Hayward House, Barnard Crescent, Aylesbury, Bucks HP21 0PG.

Brittle Bone Society, Ward 8, Strathmartine Hospital, Strathmartine, Dundee DD3 0PG.

Centre for Studies on Inclusive Education, 1 Redland Close, Elme Lane, Redland, Bristol BS6 6UE.

The Children's Society, Edward Rudolph House, Margery Street, London WC1X 0JL.

Contact-A-Family, 170 Tottenham Court Road, London W1P 0HA.

Council for Disabled Children, c/o National Children's Bureau, 8 Wakley Street, London EC1V 7QE.

Cystic Fibrosis Research Trust, Alexandra House, 5 Blyth Road, Bromley, Kent BR1 3RS.

DIAL UK, 117 High Street, Clay Cross, Derbyshire. (Nationwide telephone information and advice services)

Disability Alliance, ERA, 1st Floor East, Universal House, 88–94 Wentworth Street, London E1 7SA.

Disabled Living Foundation, 380–384 Harrow Road, London W9 2HU.

Down's Syndrome Association, 155 Mitcham Road, London SW17 9PG.

Family Fund, Joseph Rowntree Memorial Trust, PO Box 50, York YO1 1UY.

Friedreich's Ataxia Group, The Common, Cranleigh, Surrey GU8 8SB.

Greater London Association for Disabled People, 336 Brixton Road, London SW9 7AA.

Haemophilia Society, 123 Westminster Bridge Road, London SE1 7HR.

Handicapped Adventure Playground Association, Fulham Palace, Bishops Avenue, London SW6 6EA.

Huntington's Disease Association, 108 Battersea High Street, London SW11 3HP.

Hyperactive Children's Support Group, 71 Whyke Lane, Chichester, Sussex PO19 2LD.

I CAN, 4 Dyers Building, Holborn, London EC1N 2OP.

IN TOUCH, 10 Norman Road, Sale, Cheshire M33 3DF. (Information and contacts for rare handicapping conditions)

IPSEA, 22 Warren Hill Road, Woodbridge, Suffolk IP12 4DU.

KIDS, 80 Waynflete Square, London W10 6UD.

Leukaemia Care Society, PO Box 82, Exeter, Devon EX2 5DP.

MENCAP (Royal Society for Mentally Handicapped Children and Adults), 117–123 Golden Lane, London EC1Y 0RT.

MIND (National Association for Mental Health), 22 Harley Street, London W1N 2ED.

Motability, Gate House, West Gate, The High, Harlow, Essex CM10 1HR. 01279 635666.

Muscular Dystrophy Group of Great Britain, 7–11 Prescott Place, London SW4 6BS.

National Association for the Education of Sick Children, Open School, 18 Victoria Park Square, London E2 9PF.

National Association of Special Educational Needs (NASEN), Nasen House, 4–5 Amber Business Village, Amber Close, Amington, Tamworth, Staffs B77 4RP.

National Autistic Society, 276 Willesden Lane, London NW2 5RB.

National Deaf Children's Society, 45 Hereford Road, London W2 5AH.

National Eczema Society, 4 Tavistock Place, London WC1H 9RA.

National Federation of the Blind of the UK, Unity House, Smyth Street, Westgate, Wakefield, West Yorkshire WF1 1ER.

National Library for the Handicapped Child, Ash Court, Rose Street, Wokingham, Berks RG11 1XS.

National Physically Handicapped and Able Bodied, Padholme Road East, Peterborough PE1 5UL.

National Portage Association, 4 Clifton Road, Winchester, Hants. (Work with parents of young handicapped children)

National Rathbone Society, 1st Floor, Princess House, 105–107 Princess Street, Manchester M1 6DD

National Toy Libraries Association, 68 Churchway, London NW1 1LT.

NETWORK, 16 Princeton Street, London WC1R 4BB.

NETWORK 81, 1–7 Woodfield Terrace, Chapel Hill, Stansted, Essex CM24 8AJ.

Parents In Partnership, Unit 2, Ground Floor, 70 South Lambert Road, London SW8 1RL.

Pre-school Playgroup Association, 61–63 Kings Cross Road, London WC1X 9LL.

Royal Association for Disability and Rehabilitation, 12 City Forum, 250 City Road, London EC1V 8AF.

Royal National Institute for the Blind, 105 Judd Street, London WC1 9NE.

Royal National Institute for the Deaf, 105 Gower Street, London WC1E 6AH.

SCOPE (formerly known as The Spastics Society), 12 Park Crescent, London W1N 4EQ.

SENSE, 11–13 Clifton Terrace, Finsbury Park, London N4 3SR.

Sickle Cell Society, 54 Station Road, London NW10 4UA.

SKILL (formerly the National Bureau for Handicapped Students), 336 Brixton Road, London SW9 7AA.

Special Education Consortium, c/o Council for Disabled Children, 8 Wakley Street, London EC1V 7QE.

Spinal Injuries Association, Newpoint House, 76 St James Lane, London N10 3DF.

Stroke Association, CHSA House, Whitecross Street, London EC1Y 8JJ.

Tuberous Sclerosis Association of Great Britain, Martell Mount, Holywell Road, Malvern, Wells, Worcestershire WR14 4LF.

Young Minds, 22a Boston Place, London NW1 6ER.

(List reproduced from DFE 1994 document entitled *Special Educational Needs: A Guide for Parents*. This has been revised where appropriate.)

Further reading and references

HMSO/DFE and DfES publications

Audit Commission/HMI (1992a) *Getting in on the Act: A Management Handbook for Schools and LEAs*. HMSO.

Audit Commission/HMI (1992b) *Getting the Act Together*. HMSO.

The Children Act 1989. HMSO.

Children and Young People (1978) *(The Warnock Report)*. DES.

Circular 11/90, Staffing for pupils with special educational needs guidance. DFE.

DFE (1994) *Code of Practice on the Identification and Assessment of Special Educational Needs*. DFE and Welsh Office.

Excellence for All Children: Meeting Special Educational Needs. DfEE.

Disabled Person (Services Consultation and Representation) Act 1986. HMSO.

Discipline in Schools: Report of the Committee of Enquiry (1989) *(The Elton Report)*. DES/HMSO.

DfEE (2000a) *Provision for Speech and Language Therapy Services to Children with Special Educational Needs: Report of the Working Group*. DfEE.

DfEE (2000b) *SEN Thresholds: Good Practice Guidance on Identification and Provision for Pupils with Special Educational Needs*. DfEE.

DfES (2001) *SEN Toolkit*.

Education Act 1944. HMSO.

Education Act 1993. HMSO.

Education Reform Act 1988. HMSO.

Education (Special Educational Needs Code of Practice) (Appointed Day) Regulations 1994, SI 1994. HMSO.

QCA (1999) *QCA/99/458: Inclusion: Providing Effective Learning Opportunities for All*.

QCA (2000): *Planning, Teaching and Assessing the Curriculum for Pupils with Learning Difficulties*, March 2000.

SEN Tribunals: Consultative Paper on Draft Regulations and Rules of Procedure. DFE.

SEN Tribunal Regulations 1994, SI 1910. HMSO.

SEN Tribunal: how to appeal. DFE Publications Centre.

SEN Code of Practice, 2001, DfES

Special Educational Needs: a Guide for Parents, 5/94. DFE Publications Centre.

Hampshire publications

These titles have been published in Hampshire with the Code of Practice in mind and are obtainable from the Education Department Publicity Unit, The Castle, Winchester SO23 8UG.

N1 *A Guide for Schools: The SEN Code of Practice* (Newsheet).

N2 *A Guide for Schools: The Named Person and the SEN Code of Practice* (Newsheet).

L1 *What are Special Educational Needs?*

L2 *Your Young Child's Development.*

L3 *Autism.*

L4 *Portage.*

L5 *The Annual Review.*

L6 *An Audit of Special Educational Needs.*

L7 *Hampshire's Education Service and Parents in Partnership.*

L8 *The Named Person (Befriender): A Guide for Parents and Carers.*

L9 *Further Statutory Assessments: A Guide for Parents and Carers.*

Other publications

(This list comprises titles for further reading and titles referred to in the text)

Advisory Centre for Education (ACE) (1994) *Special Needs – Support for Governors*. London.

Advisory Centre for Education (ACE) (1995) *Special Education Handbook*. London.

Ainscow, M. (1991) *Effective Schools for All*. London: David Fulton Publishers.

Aldridge, T. (1995) 'Appeal in progress', *Education*, 5 May.

Allan, J. (1999): '*I don't need this: acts of transgression by students with special educational needs*', in K. Ballard (ed.) *Inclusive Education: International Voices on Disability and Justice*. London: Falmer Press.

Armstrong, F., Armstrong, D. and Barton, L. (2000) *Inclusive Education: Policy, Contexts and Comparative Perspectives*. London: David Fulton Publishers.

Bald, J. (1995) 'Integration makes the difference', *Guardian*, March.

Ballard, K. (ed.) (1999) *Inclusive Education: International Voices on Disability and Justice*. London: Falmer Press.

Barton, L. (1987) *The Politics of Special Educational Needs*. Lewes: Falmer Press.

Booth, T. (1994) 'Continua or chimera', *British Journal of Special Education* **21**(1), 21–4.

Bowers, T. (1996) *Schools, Services and Special Educational Needs*. Cambridge: Perspective Press.

Bowers, T., Dee, L. and West, M. (1998) 'The Code in action: some school perceptions of its user friendliness', *Support for Learning, British Journal of Learning Support* **13**(3), August.

Branston, P. and Provis, M. (1986) *Children and Parents Enjoy Reading*. London: Hodder and Stoughton.

Buckley, S. (2000) 'What Sara started', in K. Gold, *Times Educational Supplement*, 7 July.

Buckley, S. and Bird, G. (1994) *Meeting the Educational Needs of Children with Down's Syndrome: A Handbook for Teachers*. University of Portsmouth, Hampshire.

Carnall, C. (1989) *Managing Change*. Hemel Hempstead: Prentice Hall.

Chasty, H. and Friel, J. (1991) *Assessment Law and Practice – Caught in the Act*. London: Kingsley.

Cohen, A. and Cohen, L. (eds) (1986) *Special Educational Needs in the Ordinary School*. London: Harper and Row.

Cooper, P. (1996) 'Are Individual Education Plans a waste of paper?', *British Journal of Special Education* **23**(3), September.

Corbett, J. (1996) *Bad Mouthing: The Language of Special Needs,* London: Falmer Press.

Cornwell, N. (1987) *Statementing and the 1981 Education Act.* Bedford: Cranfield Press.

Cowne, E. (2000) *The SENCO Handbook: Working within a Whole School Approach.* 3rd ed. London: David Fulton Publishers.

Cronk, K. A. (1987) *Teacher–Pupil Conflict in Secondary Schools.* Lewes: Falmer Press.

Davies, J., Garner, P. and Lee, J. (1998) *Managing Special Needs in Mainstream Schools: the Role of the SENCO.* London: David Fulton Publishers.

Dearing, R. (1993) *Review of the National Curriculum and Its Assessment.* London: SCAA.

Denman, R. and Lunt, I. (1993) 'Getting your Act together: some implications for EPs of cases of judicial review', *Educational Psychology in Practice* **9**(1), 9–16.

Denman, R. and Lunt. I. (1995) 'More or less appealing Act', *Educational Psychology in Practice* **10**(4), 238–46.

Department for Education and Skills (DfES) (2001a) *Special Educational Needs Code of Practice.* London: DfES.

Department for Education and Skills (DfES) (2001b) *SEN Toolkit.* London: DfES.

Dunn, L. (1968) 'Special education for the mildly retarded – Is much of it justifiable', *Exceptional Children* **35**, 5–22.

Evans, A. and Tomlinson, J. (1989) *Teacher Appraisal: A Nationwide Approach.* London: Jessica Kingsley Publishers.

Faupel, A. (1994) 'Psychological assessment of children with emotional and behavioural difficulties', in J. Gross (1996).

Freshfields Litigation Team (1998) *The Woolf Reforms in Practice: Freshfields Assess the Changing Landscape.* London: Butterworths.

Galloway, D. (1976) 'Size of school, socio-economic hardship, suspension rate and persistent unjustified absence from school', *British Journal of Educational Psychology* **46**(1) 40–47.

Galloway, D. (1986) in A. Cohen and L. Cohen (eds) *Special Educational Needs in the Ordinary School.* London: Harper and Row.

Galloway, D., Armstrong, A. and Tomlinson, S. (1994) *The Assessment of Special Educational Needs: whose problem?* London: Longman.

Gersch, I. S. *et al.* (1993) 'Valuing the child's perspective: a revised student report and other practical initiatives', *Educational Psychology in Practice* **9**(1), 36–45.

Gross, J. (1996) 'The weight of the evidence: parental advocacy and resource allocation to children with Statements of Special Educational Needs, *Support for Learning* **11**(1), February.

Hannavy, S. (1995) 'Able and willing', *Special Children*, May.

Harris, N. (1997) 'Negligence, Liability and Educational Professionals', *Educational Psychology in Practice* **14**(2), July.

Hayden, C. (1997) *Children Excluded From School: Debates, Evidence, Responses,* Buckingham: Open University Press.

Ingram, J. and Worrall, N. (1993) *Teacher–Child Partnership.* London: David Fulton Publishers.

Jenkins, P. (1993) *Children's Rights.* Harlow: Longman.

Johnson, P. (1995) 'Costing the SEN Code of Practice', *Education*, 26 May.

Jones, F., Jones, K., and Szwed, C. (2001) *The SENCO as Teacher and Manager: A Guide for Practitioners and Trainers.* London: David Fulton Publishers.

Lovitt, T., Cushing, S. and Stump, C. (1994) 'High school students rate their IEPs: low opinions and lack of ownership', *Intervention in School and Clinic* **30**(1) 34–7.

Lunt, I. and Evans, J. (1994) 'Allocating resources for special educational provision', Policy Options for Special Needs. Stafford: NASEN.

Lynch, E. and Beare, P. (1990) The quality of IEP objectives and their relevance to instruction for students with mental retardation and behavioural disorders, *Remedial and Special Education* **11**(2), 48–55.

Macbeth, A. (1989) *Involving Parents*. London: Heinemann Educational.

Macready, T. (1991) 'Special education: some thoughts for policy makers', *Educational Psychology in Practice* **7**, 148–53.

Marsh, A. (1998) 'Resourcing inclusive education: the real economics', in P. Clough (ed.) *Managing Inclusive Education: From Policy To Experience*. London: Paul Chapman.

Millward, A. and Skidmore, D. (1998) 'LEA responses to the management of special education in the light of the Code of Practice', *Educational Management and Administration* **26**, 57–66.

Mittler, P. (2000) *Working Towards Inclusive Education: Social Contexts*. London: David Fulton Publishers.

Ofsted (1996) *The Implementation of the Code of Practice for Children with Special Educational Needs*. London: HMSO.

Ofsted (2002) *Annual Report of HM Chief Inspector of Schools, 2000/2001*. London: Ofsted.

Oliver, M. (1990) *The Politics of Disablement*, London: Macmillan.

Parsons, C. (2000) *Investigating the Reintegration of Permanently Excluded Young People in England*. Cambridge: INCLUDE.

Peter, M. (1995) 'Trends in law: fifteen years of education policy making, 1979–94', in P. Potts, F. Armstrong and M. Masterton, *Equality and Diversity in Education, Vol. 2*. Milton Keynes: Open University.

Potts, P., Armstrong, F. and Masterton, M. (1995) *Equality and Diversity in Education, Vols. 1 and 2*. Milton Keynes: Open University.

Ramjhun, A. (1995) *Implementing the Code of Practice for Children with Special Educational Needs*, London: David Fulton Publishers.

Ramjhun, A. (2001) 'Rhetoric and Reality of Inclusion: An Examination of Policy and Practice in Southampton LEA', unpublished Doctor of Education Thesis, Milton Keynes, The Open University.

Reynolds, D. (1976) 'The delinquent school', in M. Hammersley, and P. Woods (eds), pp. 58, 85, 93–4.

Reynolds, D. (1995) 'Using school effectiveness knowledge for children with special educational needs: the problems and possibilities', in C. Clark, A. Dyson and A. Millwood, *Towards Inclusive Schools?* London: David Fulton Publishers.

Reynolds, D. and Murgatroyd, D. S. (1979) 'The sociology of schooling and the absent pupil: the school as a factor in the generation of truancy', in H. C. M. Carroll (ed.) *Absenteeism in South Wales: Studies of pupils, their homes and their secondary schools*. Swansea: Faculty of Education, University of Swansea.

Riddell, S., Brown, S. and Duffield J. (1999) 'Parental power and SEN: the case of specific learning difficulties', *British Educational Research Journal* **20**, 327–44.

Robinson, J. (1994) 'Special educational needs after the 1993 reforms', *Education and the Law* **6**(1), 3–14.

Russell, P. (1994) 'The Code of Practice: new partnerships for children with special educational needs', *British Journal of Special Education* **21**(2), 48–52.

Rutter, M. and Madge, N. (1981) *Cycles of Disadvantage*. London: Heinemann.

Rutter, M., Maughan, B., Mortimore, P. and Ouston, J. (1979) *Fifteen Thousand Hours: secondary schools and their effects on children*. London: Open Books.

SCC (1998) *Promoting Inclusion: Children Experiencing Learning Difficulties*. Southampton: Southampton City Council.

SCC (1999) *Promoting Inclusion: Children Experiencing Emotional and Behavioural Difficulties*. Southampton: Southampton City Council.

School Curriculum and Assessment Authority (1994) *Dearing: The Final Report*. London: SCAA.

Scott, L. (June, 1994) *Special Needs: Support for Governors*. Advisory Centre for Education (ACE).

SEN Tribunal (1994/5) *Annual Report*. London: SEN Tribunal.

SEN Tribunal (1995/6) *Annual Report*. London: SEN Tribunal.

SEN Tribunal (1996/7) *Annual Report*. London: SEN Tribunal.

SEN Tribunal (1997/8) *Annual Report*. London: SEN Tribunal.

SEN Tribunal (1998/9) *Annual Report*. London: SEN Tribunal.

SEN Tribunal (1999/2000) *Annual Report*. London: SEN Tribunal.

Sigafoos, J., Elkins, J., Couzens, D., Gunn, S., Roberts, D. and Kerr, M. (1993) 'Analysis of IEP goals and classroom activities for children with multiple disabilities', *European Journal of Special Needs Education* 8(2), 99–105.

Simmons, K. (1994) 'Decoding a new message', *British Journal of Special Education* 21(9), 56–9.

Skrtic, T. (1991) in M. Ainscow, *Effective Schools for All*. London: David Fulton Publishers.

Special Children (1995a) 'Tribunal hit by rush of appeals', March issue.

Special Children (1995b) 'High Court case new blow to tribunal', April issue.

Times Educational Supplement (1994) 'Lawyers getting ready for big boom in business when Special Needs Tribunals arrive in September', 25 February.

Tizard, B. and Hughes, M. (1984) *Young Children Learning*. London: Fontana.

Tizard, B., Schofield, W. N. and Hewison, J. (1982) 'Collaboration between teachers and parents in assisting children's reading', *British Journal of Educational Psychology* 52(1), 1–15.

Topping, K. and Wolfendale, S. (eds) (1985) *Parental Involvement in Children's Reading*. London: Croom Helm.

Utting, W. (1997) *People Like Us: The Report of the Safeguards for Children Living Away from Home*, Department of Health. London: The Stationery Office.

Vevers, P. (1992) 'Getting in on the Act', *British Journal of Special Education* 9(3), 88–91.

Ware, J. (1994) *Educating Children with Profound and Multiple Learning Difficulties*. London: David Fulton Publishers.

Wolfendale, S. (1988) 'The parental contribution to assessment', *Developing Horizons 10*. Available from NCSE, 1 Wood Street, Stratford-upon-Avon CV37 6JF.

Wolfendale, S. (ed.) (1989) *Parental Involvement: Developing Networks between Home, School and Community*. London: Cassell.

Wolfendale, S. (1992) *Empowering Parents and Teachers*. London: Cassell.

Woolf, Lord (1995) *Access to Justice: Interim Report to the Lord Chancellor on the Civil Justice System in England and Wales*, London: Lord Chancellor's Office.

Wright, J. (1994) 'Promises, promises', *Special Children* 71, 11–12.

Wright, J. (1995) 'From Bill to Act: the passing of the 1993 Education Act', in P. Potts, F. Armstrong and M. Masterton *Equality and Diversity in Education*, *Vol. 2*. Milton Keynes: Open University.

Index